To Cousin Alissa,
Enjoy the "oy!"
Love, Ellie

Mishegas of Motherhood

Raising Children to Leave the Nest
As Long As They Come Home for Dinner

By Ellie S. Grossman

ISBN: 978-1-891442-71-1

Bluebird Publishing Co.
PO Box 4538
St. Louis, MO 63108
www.bluebirdbookpub.com

More Praise for
Mishegas of Motherhood

"In the past, after reading the front page of the newspaper, I normally turn to the wedding and obits as most people my age probably do. I don't do that anymore. I go straight to *Mishegas of Motherhood*. The columns are insightful and thought provoking. They make me want to dust off the old Royal from journalism school and hunt and peck away, waxing as eloquently as you do about subjects that all of us have experienced in the human condition."
—Rick Hitt, St. Louis, MO

"You are wise and your writing is wonderful, just full of practical wisdom and insights....I loved the article about finding God in the ordinary experiences of our daily lives. I think you and I are cut from the same cloth!"
—Becky Cawley, Melbourne, FL

"I just had a laughing attack in the bathtub while reading your camping trip story. It felt great—thanks! I would pay BIG money to have a good chuckle on a daily basis, or perhaps I will just wait for you to send one my way. Do you have a fan club yet?"
—Terri Wright, St. Louis, MO

"You tickle my soul girl! You have such an incredible gift. Your joy reflects in your work, and I just love it."
—Stephanie Gessner, St. Louis, MO

Mishegas of Motherhood
Raising Children to Leave the Nest
As Long As They Come Home for Dinner

I dedicate this book to Jack and Sari,
who still think I do nothing all day long
while they're at school.

Acknowledgements

To my husband Scott, who understands that when he rolls over in bed at 3 a.m. and I'm gone, I'm either outside in my pajamas walking the dog or in the office staring at the computer.

To my mom Charlotte, whose advice I ignored when she said, "You're too busy to write a book now. Wait until after the kids are away at college, and then you'll have more time."

To my children Jack and Sari, who fill my life with *mishegas* and give my words a purpose. No matter how old you are, I'll always peel the apple skins for you.

To my toy poodle Luci, who never talks back to me and doesn't expect an allowance when I ask her to bring me the newspaper.

Last but not least, to Wendy Mogel, Ph.D., author of *The Blessing of a Skinned Knee*, whose interpretation of Jewish teachings has inspired many writings in my book.

Introduction

I kept a journal throughout my first pregnancy, so I started to write about my experiences as a mom before my first child was even born. While I was in labor, in fact, I grabbed my notebook and pen in between contractions in my hospital bed and scrawled random thoughts as quickly as I could. One line reads, "The potocin is dripping into my veins and the pain is getting BAAAAAAAD!" Another entry begins, "My mother is serving homemade *kamish* bread to my Ob/Gyn, and all I can do is suck on ice chips..."

In the early days as a working mom and newspaper reporter for the *St. Louis Post Dispatch*, I toted my redheaded toddler Jack to many of my assignments, including when I reviewed story times at local bookstores. I have fond memories of sitting cross-legged with my son on sticky, carpeted floors, listening to books like, *If You Give a Pig a Pancake*, while I guzzled mocha lattes and Jack crunched on rice cakes.

Now Jack is 16 and driving, and my daughter Sari is 12 and about to become a *bat mitzvah*. Funny how they get older and I stay the same age. When Jack was 11 and Sari was 7, I started to chronicle the *mishegas*, or craziness, of my life. The chronicles became a regular column, *Mishegas of Motherhood*, for *The St. Louis Jewish Light*. This book is a compilation of my favorite entries.

In writing *Mishegas*, I discovered how much Judaism and parenting go hand in hand and that the time-tested wisdom of the ancient sages can teach us a lot about contemporary child rearing. But I also learned that the themes of motherhood are universal and resonate with parents of all denominations, not just Jewish ones, especially when it comes to talking to our children about God, trying to keep mealtime sacred, teaching the importance of community service, and hiding in a heated mini van at an overnight family campout (see Chapter 12 for that gem).

Let's face it. Motherhood and parenting are full of *mishegas*, no matter what religion or culture you are. If you're a parent, you share in the craziness. Welcome aboard!

This book is a journey. It's an exploration of the oys and joys of parenting that we all share. So, I invite you to kick back, microwave a cup of jasmine tea, and share a few good laughs and insights inspired by my own *mishegas*. If nothing else, it'll get you out of folding the laundry for an hour or two.

Ellie S. Grossman
St. Louis, MO
September 2011

Chapter 1
In The Beginning...There Was God, And There Was Mom

A Labor Of Love Debuts

When I was a student in journalism school in the mid 1980s, I had the privilege of meeting the famous humorist Erma Bombeck. Actually, I yelled a question to her from the back row of a packed lecture hall at the University of Missouri School of Journalism. I raised my hand high in the air and yelled out, "How do you deal with writer's block?" Obviously, she had been asked this question many times before, because right on cue she said, "Writer's block is like North Dakota. It doesn't exist." Then she broke up the burst of laughter with: "Well, has anyone ever *been* to North Dakota?"

Now I get what she means. When I began writing my column *Mishegas of Motherhood* for *The St. Louis Jewish Light* in 2006, my son Jack was 11 and my daughter Sari was 7 going on 17. I always had something to write about and, thanks to my Jewish faith, I always had a prayer to cling to.

As I raise my children in a public school where they're a minority, I try to plant roots of Judaism whenever I can, and I'm about as reformed as they come. I know this makes a difference because Sari used to insist that the stars on her math papers in elementary school were Jewish ones. And her favorite food is Great Grandma Ruth's cabbage borscht. The fact that Jack walks around the house chanting the V'ahavta—for the fun of it—makes me think that he knows he is a Jew and is proud of it. The ways that I try to reinforce their Jewish identity go way beyond dragging them out of bed on Sunday mornings for religious school. It's the little extras that we do as a family now and then to remember we are special, that we are Jews.

For example, on Rosh Hashanah, especially on a beautiful fall day, we try to take a fun outing to a neighborhood park and perform the ritual of tashlich by casting away our "sins" in a big lake with floating ducks. Then we go to Subway for a turkey sandwich, but that's beside the point.

As my kids become teenagers and the pressures of parenthood continually change, I sometimes find myself looking elsewhere for answers to everyday battles, like how to get everyone to sit down at the dinner table at the same time and actually swallow our food before someone jumps up to go somewhere.

I recently discovered that many insights to raising children are found not on the Dr. Phil show but in the teachings in the Torah, the Talmud, and the writings of the ancient sages. What do rabbis and scholars from centuries ago know about the hassles of the carpool line, the challenges of balancing good grades with batting practice, or the latest trend to hire professional motivators for extravagant bar mitzvahs? A lot, it turns out. In fact, the most time-tested advice on modern parenting struggles, from over scheduling kids to the focus on materialism, comes from the insights of the learned Jewish thinkers.

Especially in today's fast-paced and complex world, the Jewish lessons that command us to slow down and savor the moment, which is the purpose of Shabbat, have never seemed more appropriate. Way before *Supernanny* came along, Jewish parents followed these invaluable words of wisdom for thousands of years. Our parents and grandparents were on to this already.

The Fifth Commandment—Honor Thy Father and Mother—is a good place to start, don't you think?

Honor Thy Father And Mother

Before David Letterman had his Top 10 list, God made the original Top 10, as in Commandments. Coming in at number five—Honor Thy Father and Mother— is key to raising self-reliant children.

Obviously, God was serious about parental respect. Not until I had children of my own, however, did I truly appreciate this logic. In fact, I swore I'd never say things like "Because I said so" when my kids would ask me why they can't stay up 30 minutes past their bedtime. Sometimes I give such lengthy explanations they forget their original question.

For example, I might ramble, "You need to go to bed right now because you had a sleepover the other night, and you were up really late, and you need to be well rested for your spelling test tomorrow, and besides if you don't get enough sleep you will be sick, and you don't want to miss your best friend's birthday party at Chuck E. Cheese's."

This surely exhausts them, as they cover their heads with pillows to block out the sound of my voice.

The philosophy here is to teach kids early on who is the boss and to be consistent until they leave the nest. Ah, if only it were that easy.

Many parents in my generation give their kids a say in everything, maybe because they feel guilty for not spending quality time with them. The truth is, my children don't need me as a friend. They need a role model to look up to, an authority figure who isn't a wimp when it comes to saying no. Judaism says the best place to start is respect, or teaching the virtue of *derech eretz*, or the way of the land, by emphasizing good old-fashioned manners, like saying "please" and "thank you" and, of course, wiping the toilet seat.

Then again, parents have to pick their battles, and one of my biggest pet peeves is when Sari calls me by my first name, Ellie. She only yells it out in "emergencies," such as when she freaks out about a tornado siren, when Luci, our toy poodle, chews another napkin out of the trash, or when she can't find her favorite white sandals with the flowers. The last time she hollered "Ellie" I calmly explained to her that children don't call their parents by their first names because it doesn't show respect. I warned her that the next time she calls me Ellie I'll ignore her, even if a funnel cloud is overhead. I went on to suggest more appropriate titles, such as mom, mommy, mama, Ima, or even mother dearest. There I go again with the choices—another weakness of mine.

We often teach what we need to learn, and the lesson to honor God starts with respecting ourselves and each other. As always, this takes a lot of time and energy.

Answering The Big Question: Is There A God?

One of the most significant passages into parenthood is when your child innocently asks you the BIG question—the one Jewish parents plotz over because they fear that if they don't answer it perfectly, their child will wind up in therapy.

For many of us, the question "Is there a God?" raises more anxiety than the birds-and-bees conversation. For me, these significant bonding moments usually occur when I least expect it, like while I'm driving down Interstate 64 with Jack and Sari in tow and trying to search for a Neil Diamond CD and hand sanitizer all at the same time.

The other day, another serious discussion about God took place as I raced my kids to Sunday school. I turned down the volume on *Sweet Caroline* for a conversation that went something like this:

Sari: "I don't think there is a God."
Me: "Why not?"
Sari: "Because there's no proof. People always look up to the sky when they think about God, but I don't believe that God is up there."
Jack: "So you don't believe in God?"
Sari: "I didn't say that."
Jack: "Yes you did. I just heard you say that you don't believe in God. Now you are lying."
Sari: "MOOOOOM, Jack is making fun of me."
Me: "Come on Jack, let your sister explain how she feels. We are lucky to be Jewish because our religion gives us permission to wonder about God. Go ahead Sari and finish your thought."
Sari: "What I mean is I don't believe God is a person. I don't believe that God is in heaven. I don't even know what heaven is. I don't believe God is in a flower either."
Me: "I believe that God made a miracle when he made you."
Sari: "God didn't make me. You and daddy did."

Oops, I forgot we already had that talk.

At least the answer to how babies are born is black and white, cut and dried, and science backs it up. The proof of

God, on the other hand, is not found in a lab, but in the Ten Commandments. Therefore, the concept of God is more challenging and can be taught in many ways, including in the magical Jewish Bible stories that pack more action than Harry Potter and Power Rangers combined. Not even Steven Spielberg could come up with a plot as unforgettable as turning the waters of the Nile into blood.

Another way to teach about God is through our actions. For Sari, I show my love when we snuggle together under my purple down comforter and we laugh at home movies of her when she was a baby. When she has a cold and feels yucky, I make her a cozy spa in my bathroom complete with a bubble bath, aromatherapy candles, ocean sounds, and a warm cup of sweet green tea.

For Jack, I show my love and God's example when I tuck a brand new baseball card under his pillow after he loses a tooth, even though he doesn't believe in the tooth fairy anymore. And when he sometimes practices his favorite sport with me, I let his fast ball smack into my oversized leather glove and sting my hand.

Our conversation on the road continues:

Me: "Sari, can you see love?"
Sari: "No, but I love my family and our dog."
Me: "Even though you can't see love, you know it's real, right?"
Sari: "Well, yeah, I feel love in my heart."
Me: "Exactly. God is like love, something you can't see with your eyes or hear with your ears, but something you feel in your heart."

Then I hear silence. As I pull into the temple parking lot, I look in the rearview mirror and smile as Sari peels a banana for her older brother in the backseat. After I drop them off and start to clean up the banana peels and juice boxes off the floor,

I reflect on the last 20 minutes of enlightenment and realize how easy I got off this time. As my kids get older and struggle with existential questions about the reasons why another child disappears off the street or why a suicide bomber destroys a crowded coffee shop in Tel Aviv, our conversations about God will get even juicier.

A medieval proverb says, "If I knew God, I would be God." In other words, I don't need to know the "right" answers in order to talk to my children about God. Perhaps the best part about being a parent is that it gives me an excuse to continue learning.

When In Doubt, Do As The Jews Do

When the Sunday school teacher asks the second graders to draw a picture of what God means to them, most of the students grab their colored markers and eagerly get to work. They waste no time making bright rainbows, beautiful flowers, puffy clouds, beaming sunshine, twinkling stars, and an assortment of bearded stick figures. I join other parents in the classroom, and I witness firsthand how the topic of God sparks creativity in grownups and children alike. Everyone seems to enjoy the opportunity to explore God out loud; everyone, that is, except my daughter.

Not surprising to me, Sari is the only one who stares at a blank piece of paper for what feels like forever. I fidget in my chair and smile, waiting for Sari to snap out of her spell. I tap her knee under the table and ask, "What's wrong? Why aren't you making a picture like everyone else?"

"I don't know what to draw," Sari whispers in my ear, "because I don't know what God is. What if I don't believe in God because there's no proof?"

Here we go again, I think to myself. Can't anything be easy? For God's sake (no pun intended), this art project is supposed to be fun.

"Draw anything," I tell her impatiently. "The first thing that jumps into your mind when you think of God, put it down on paper."

Instead, she leans her elbows on the table and cradles her face in her hands. She appears to be in deep thought, waiting for inspiration. Either that or she's playing a game with my nerves. I get restless as the teacher starts to collect the drawings and the hungry artists head for the snack table.

Finally, I tell her, "There's no right or wrong answer here, honey. This isn't a MAP test like at school. Plus, if you don't finish your picture our favorite fudge brownies will disappear."

Thankfully, the creative juices stir and Sari scribbles question marks and polka dots in different colors and sizes all over the white paper. She might be the last one to hand in her assignment, but I'm relieved nevertheless. Still, I worry that the teacher might think Sari's rendition of a higher being is not "Jewish enough." Fortunately, the teacher compliments her drawing and tells Sari that she appreciates her honesty. Good answer.

Truth is, questioning the existence of God has been built into Jewish theology since, well, the very beginning. In fact, the word *Yisrael* literally means "person who struggles with God."

As Sari gets ready for bed later that night and smears Colgate on her toothbrush, she brings up the subject of God again. "Why do I always have to draw pictures and write about God at religious school?" she asks. "I'm getting tired of the whole thing."

I rub a big towel in her wet hair and challenge her right back: "Why do you always ask me questions that I have no definite answers to?"

After a few minutes of silence, I realize that I actually do have an answer. "You know, since you're a Jew, you don't have to believe in God, but you do have to *be*."

Sari looks confused as she wipes the toothpaste off her chin. So I add, "You're still a good Jew even if you're not sure about God, and I love you no matter what." We smile at each other in the mirror.

We continue to talk as I tuck my sleepy daughter under her fleece blanket and squeeze in beside her. "The ancient rabbis tell us that it's perfectly okay not to believe in God or Adam and Eve or even the story about how Moses parts the Red Sea," I said. "But these wise teachers from a very long time ago still ask us to live a Jewish life anyway. That means you can doubt God all you want, but you still have to celebrate the Jewish holidays, practice the rituals, give *tzedakah*, and learn about our history."

Sari doesn't say anything. Is she speechless for once or sound asleep already? Then she rolls over and I hear, "Good night, mommy. I love you."

I close my eyes and take in this special moment. It doesn't happen very often. I wonder how Sari will discover God as she gets older and wiser. Maybe she'll feel God's warmth when she lights a Shabbat candle. Maybe she'll hear God's voice in nature when she waves the *lulav* in the *sukkah*. Maybe she'll taste God's tears when she dips her pinkie in a cup of wine at the Passover seder. Maybe she'll see God's miracle when she becomes a mother and looks into her newborn's eyes for the first time.

Chapter 2
Just When You Think You Haven't Got A Prayer

The Value Of Prayer

When it comes to prayers, Jews have it covered. We have a prayer for everything—from the morning ritual *Modeh Ani*, which thanks God for returning our soul to us, to the bedtime blessing *Shema Yisrael*. In addition to the traditional blessings over food and the holidays, special prayers can be learned for each gift that God gives us throughout the day. For example, there's a prayer for when we wear new clothes for the first time, hear a booming thunderstorm, smell the fragrant scent of a magnolia blossom, reunite with a long-lost friend, and so on. Even when we notice a strange-looking person or animal, we can say, "Blessed are You, Lord our God, who varies creation…"

Observant Jews pray in formal worship services three times a day, every day. But even if we aren't Orthodox Jews and our knowledge of Jewish liturgy is limited to the High Holidays in synagogue and an occasional Shabbat dinner at home, we still have plenty of opportunities through our children to make prayer part of our everyday lives.

In fact, prayer is an excellent way to instill values in children and increase their awareness of God all around them. All prayers start with *"Baruch Atah Adonai, Eloheinu Melach Ha'olam,"* which translates to "Blessed are You, Lord our God, Ruler of the Universe," then we add the specific prayer for each of life's pleasures.

For example, when we pick the season's first ripe peach and bite into the sweet, juicy flesh, we say the *Shehecheyanu,* the prayer for special moments. *"Shehecheyanu vekiyemanu vehigi'anu lazman hazeh,"* which means, "Who has given us life, sustained us, and enabled us to reach this time."

When we delight in the colorful arch of a rainbow, we say, *"Zocher habrit, vene'eman bevrito, vekayam et maamaro,"* which means, "Who remembers the covenant (with Noah) and is faithful to the covenant and loyal to the promise."

When my family gazes at the glorious golden sunset that melts into the ocean at Siesta Beach, we appreciate how God paints the sky reddish orange by reciting *"Oseh maaseh veresheet,"* which means, "Who makes the wonders of creation."

In other words, prayer is not something that we surrender to just when life gets rough. For Jews, prayer is a daily exercise for the soul. In order to fully understand and appreciate our gratitude to God, we must train our whole lives through study and practice. Otherwise, it's like playing in the World Series without ever having thrown a baseball. Judaism also teaches us not to just recite the prayers, but be a blessing through our actions.

For me, the inspiration to "be" Jewish comes from my children. I witness how prayer connects them to their faith and empowers them to feel like they have a sense of control in a world that is often uncontrollable, not to mention a hands-on way for children to cope with their worries and fears.

When she was 7, Sari asked me to post a *mezuzah* in her bedroom. The dream-catcher that she made out of a web of yarn failed to chase away her nightmares and she asked for a prayer to help her feel safer. She may not fully understand the words written on the tiny, parchment scroll that is tucked inside the *mezuzah*, but that's okay for now. If the magic of a Jewish prayer helps my daughter sleep through the night, I'm eternally thankful.

Likewise, when he was 11, Jack reached for the healing prayer *Mi she-berakah* when his uncle was sick in the hospital. Jack prays in Hebrew for the same reason that the Talmud stresses the importance of praying in the original Jewish language.

"When I read a prayer in Hebrew, whether it's the *V'ahavta* or *Avot* I feel like I'm talking directly to God," Jack said. "When I think of prayers, I think of Hebrew and not words in English."

Hebrew links Jews all over the world. Another thing that brings Jews together is song. Many Jews, including my own son,

My family at Siesta Beach in Sarasota, FL, March 2007.

agree that when we sing or chant the blessings, we get into the proper meditative state. For Jack, who also loves hip-hop music, the melody helps him learn and eventually memorize the prayers.

"I always know what's coming next when I chant a prayer in Hebrew, which is helpful if I get lost or flip a page accidentally. Plus, singing prayers is more fun," Jack said, as he dangled upside down on the couch and jammed on his air guitar. "Hebrew rocks!"

So move over Dr. Seuss, and make room for a few children's prayer books in your home library. You never know when you'll need a prayer to turn to.

A League Of Their Own

Like so many families whose kids are involved in multiple sports and activities, the soccer field has become my home away from home lately. In fact, I relax in my nylon stadium chair more often than my leather couch at home. A typical Saturday morning soccer game starts out this way: First, I pull out and set up all the chairs. Second, I play musical lawn chairs until everyone enjoys an unobstructed view of the action. Next, I grab bottled waters from the cooler and arrange a beverage in each cup holder. Then, I serve hungry fans handfuls of sunflower seeds, even though we just gobbled chocolate donuts for breakfast. Finally, by half time, I plop myself down and ask, "What's the score?"

Both Jack and Sari love to play all kinds of sports. As a parent, I see how their favorite pastimes build self-confidence, encourage teamwork, promote health and fitness, and flourish new friendships. Most of all, these athletic programs teach children invaluable life lessons, such as how to win and how to lose. And, in my neck of the woods, where Catholic-affiliated organizations dominate competitive soccer, team sports can also introduce youngsters to religious tolerance.

As the only Jewish player on her team, Sari is truly in a league of her own. Not only is she the only second grader on the St. Alban's Strikers who is not afraid to block the ball with her knees clenched together but apparently she is the only player who feels awkward in a prayer circle. Sure, Sari always plays by the rules and has a great time with her coaches and teammates from school. So she joins hands with all the other pony-tailed girls in a big circle. When the rest of them bow their heads to pray, Sari says she daydreams or holds her head up high and is in her own thoughts. Judaism, by the way, doesn't have a specific prayer for sports, other than the one that asks God for comfort in a dangerous situation or the Sh'ma, which covers it all and is an easy one to memorize. I suggest to Sari that she can make up her own prayer because we all appreciate a little help from above sometimes.

In Catholic leagues, athletic prayers before a soccer match are common practice, and they are usually innocent enough. A typical prayer asks God for protection over the players and encourages good sportsmanship. An example of an athletic prayer is: "Most loving God, watch over all who are part of today's game—players, coaches and fans. May this day be a source of enjoyment for all who are here, whether we win or lose…"

Furthermore, references to God are typically along the lines of Loving God, Heavenly Father, Almighty God and Father, and Holy God. On occasion, however, a coach sneaks in the J-word, Jesus. Like many Jews, that's when Sari gets as defensive as a goalie at the net. She is really thrown for a loop when they end the minute-long prayer session with the "Father, Son, Holy Ghost" gesture.

When my exhausted goalie asks me after the game why the other players make the sign of the cross, I take advantage of the opportunity to talk about how Jesus fits into Judaism. I know she's not in the mood for a sermon on the Old Testament versus the Christian New Testament, like I could give one anyway. Instead, I try to keep it simple and share my Jewish belief that Jesus was a real person and a great teacher. The difference is that Jews don't pray to Jesus. We don't believe that Jesus is the Messiah. In fact, Jesus is simply not a part of our religion and so we have no need to pray to him. Instead, when Jews pray, we go directly to the top. We pray to God.

As Sari unstraps her sweaty shin guards and kicks off her muddy cleats in the garage, I realize that her experience in the prayer circle is an eye-opening lesson in Jewish pride that she'll never forget. Furthermore, I tell her that what makes a great Jewish athlete is not always what you do, but what you don't do. To illustrate my point, I tell her about the Jewish baseball player Sandy Koufax, the Hall of Fame pitcher who refused to play a World Series game back in 1965 because it fell on the holiest day of the year, Yom Kippur. "Now that's a winner," I tell her. "Hit the shower!"

God's Wake-Up Call

The memorable sound of the *shofar* is a highlight of Rosh Hashanah, especially for children who wait patiently through the songs and prayers of the service. As a young girl growing up in a reformed temple, my signal was the sharp, loud sound of the ancient ram's horn. It told me that the service was almost over, which meant that I could finally eat bobka and change out of my itchy dress.

Today, I still look forward to hearing the first blast of *tekiah*, but for a much different reason. Now that I have children of my own, the unique sounds of the *shofar* represent a new beginning of, not an end to, something special. It's a new school year, a new season, and a new opportunity to improve myself.

Not until I reached parenthood did I begin to truly understand the season of renewal and that Rosh Hashanah symbolizes much more than apples and honey. The *shofar*, which is the oldest musical instrument still in use, is a wake-up call to parents. With each blast, the *shofar* reminds us to better appreciate our children and our relationships because they seem to change faster than the red and gold leaves on autumn's sugar maples.

With one long blast of *tekiah*, God brings us together and announces: "Wake up all you sleepy heads! Today is a special day! It's a New Year! Open your ears! Pay close attention to the voice of the *shofar* and let the sound guide you to tune into the words and needs of your children!"

Then, with nine short blasts of *shevarim*, God asks: "Look inside yourselves. What were the low moments in your life this past year? What were the highs?"

Next, with three short blasts of *teruah*, God reminds us: "Again, reach deeper into your souls. Who did you hurt this past year? How can you make it better?"

Finally, with one long blast of *tekiah gadolah*, God smiles upon us and declares: "At this moment, Jews everywhere enjoy the sound of the *shofar*—the joyful song within each of you. What is your birthday wish for the world? What is your involvement in the perfection of the world?"

According to the rabbis, the 10 days between Rosh Hashanah and Yom Kippur are one of the four times during the year that the world is judged. Unlike other Jewish holidays that are connected with historical or natural events, the Days of Awe are purely religious and are a time for heartfelt introspection and serious goal setting. For children, this Jewish concept of redemption might seem over the top, but the ritual of *tashlich*, which means to "throw" or "cast off," conveys this High Holiday message loud and clear.

Most kids learn best by doing, and *tashlich*, which dates back to the Middle Ages, is a perfect activity to involve your whole family, no matter what their age. In the *tashlich* ceremony, my husband Scott and I take Jack and Sari to a neighborhood lake to throw breadcrumbs or stale matzo pieces into the water. The ceremony is symbolic and concrete at the same time, as we make a special effort to ask and grant forgiveness to loved ones and friends.

Tashlich is a wonderful way for my family to spend time together outdoors and enjoy the crisp, cool air. As we stand at the water's edge and cast our "sins" into the "depths of the sea," as described in the *Micah*, we take turns saying a prayer. Whether we write our own words or borrow them from a Jewish text, the prayer becomes our personal family service. For example:

Me: "The water is pure and teaches us that it's time to cleanse ourselves and wash away all of our mistakes."
Scott: "Today, as we throw away our bread crumbs, let us rid ourselves of all bad habits and grudges that we may have."
Jack: "Today we begin a new year of goodness. We hope that God will overlook our failings during the past year and give us another chance."
Sari: "May we always feel God's love for us and know that God will help us improve ourselves in this New Year."

On that note, I wish everyone *"L'shanah Tova Tikatatyvu,"* a traditional greeting that means, "May you be inscribed for a good New Year."

Fasting Feeds The Soul

Whoever says that wearing white after Labor Day is a fashion faux pas must not be Jewish. During the fall holiday season, white clothing is actually encouraged at Yom Kippur services because it symbolizes purity. Notice the rabbi's special white robe. Also acceptable on the holiest day of the year are sneakers and flip-flops! Never again will I balk at Sari's white sandals or force Jack to squeeze into leather loafers that are two sizes too small.

The reason that children and adults wear non-leather shoes on Yom Kippur, by the way, is because the synthetic variety makes us feel more humble. After all, the Day of Atonement is all about feeling humble. During this 24-hour fasting period, we are to abstain from food, drink, bathing, deodorant, perfume, leather shoes, and sex. That's because on Yom Kippur we relinquish the comforts and pleasures of the flesh. For many women, giving up bread for a day is a major sacrifice.

The tradition of fasting on Yom Kippur is not designed as a punishment but as a physical expression of cleansing and gives us an entire day to focus on how we relate to other people, to the world, to our self, and to God. To cram this practice of self-evaluation and atonement into one day is impossible, which is why we are supposed to use the past 10 days to practice the three T's: *teffilah* (prayer), *teshuvah* (repentance), and *tzedakah* (justice and charity). By doing our homework—and no cheating—Jewish lore tells us that we will be "written and sealed" for a good year in a celestial Book of Life.

Like any good parent, God wants us to set goals and strive to be our very best. God gives us Yom Kippur so that we can reach our highest potential, and, in the process, improve our world (*tikkun olam*). The best way for parents to teach these moral concepts to our children is by being good role models. If we show tolerance, patience, ethical concern, and forgiveness throughout the year, our children are more likely to develop these character traits, or *middot*.

In my family, communication is sometimes easier to initiate through written words rather than through verbal expression. When my children were younger, they solved more than one conflict by slipping notes to each other (and me) underneath a closed bedroom door. Usually somebody's tears turned into laughter.

During the month of *Elul*, we play a similar game of communication called "family mailbox," in which we write each other personal messages. Our family mailbox is a desktop letter holder. The idea is to stop and think about what we might have said or done to hurt someone's feelings, and then apologize with the intention of making the situation better next time. I never know what's going to be in the mail. The other day I received an anonymous letter that simply read, "I love you!" I wrote back, "Return to sender."

The Jewish Halloween?

Halloween is one of my favorite childhood holidays. Even to this day, the best part remains my guiltless binge on bite-size candy bars. Even though I don't dress up like a scary witch with frizzy black hair anymore (at least not on purpose), I still like to welcome the full harvest moon with spirit. To put my family in the mood for the upcoming winter holiday season, I decorate my home with glowing jack-o'-lanterns, scented candles, and dangling graham cracker character ornaments that seem to multiply each year.

The only other holiday that even comes close to the excitement of costume parades and candy exchanges is Purim, but the festive commemoration of evil Haman's defeat doesn't happen until the spring. By the way, the differences between the American holiday of Halloween and the Jewish celebration of Purim are significant. For starters, Halloween glorifies death, as in ghosts and goblins, which is a grim thought, but have you seen some of the frightening costumes lately? Purim, on the other hand, celebrates life with rowdy parties and a meaningful story about the survival of the Jews of ancient Persia.

Also, on the eve of All Saints' Day, children revel in tricks, pranks, and superstitions, while Purim teaches the lesson of *mishloah manot*, or making gift baskets for friends, family, and those in need. Finally, the masks we wear on these two holidays are night and day. On Halloween, many of us disguise our true selves behind gruesome faces, whereas on Purim, Jews reveal their inner souls, called *pinimius*, and let it all hang out with uninhibited dancing and rounds of schnapps.

Ironically, Jewish families who live in secular communities like mine probably participate in the customs of Halloween more than they do Purim. Perhaps that's because Halloween, just like Christmas and even Hanukkah, has become so commercialized. In fact, for many people, the popularity of Halloween ranks right up there with the belief in Santa Claus himself.

When the holidays become big business, the religious significance gets lost, and Halloween is no exception. With Halloween, the religious influences have pretty much disappeared like an apparition, at least among the general population. Halloween, which actually means the evening before All Hallows or All Saints' Day, originated in the eighth century when the Roman Catholic Church decided to honor the sanctity of all saints. The ancient pagan rites that go along with Halloween also focus on witches, sorcerers, and evil spirits, which make for good storytelling at haunted houses.

The truth is, on a drizzly Halloween night, I'm not thinking about theology when I watch Sari-the-Jester and Jack-the-Jock run ahead of me and ring more doorbells in one night than the Avon Lady does in a lifetime. Instead, I'm thinking about how I can sneak smashed Whoppers from the bottom of one of their heavy pillowcases without them finding out.

I'm not thinking about any Druid symbolism of sacred cats when I admire an adorable trick-or-treater with black-painted whiskers and long, curly tail. Instead, I'm admittedly jealous of any mom who makes her kid's costume, while I overpay for a piece of nylon that falls apart by the time we leave our driveway.

As I carry a flashlight in one hand and a video camera in the other, I'm not thinking about Celtic beliefs of sinful souls and animal sacrifice. Instead, I'm worried that the chili I made for dinner is boiling over the stove by now.

I'm not thinking about the pagan New Year's feast in which ghosts supposedly dress in costumes and hang around the tables of food or when they roam the roads with fairies on Halloween night and curdle milk, among other mischievous acts. Instead, I'm feeling melancholy because Jack, at 11, will probably outgrow this trick-or-treat tradition next year and memories of him dressed as an orange-headed baby pumpkin are preserved in a photo album. At least Sari still shares my enthusiasm about Halloween. And when she gets too old to pretend she's Pocahontas, I'll dress my little dog Luci as a pirate.

The Joys Of Oys!

Yiddish is becoming a lost language, so any effort to preserve the dialect of our ancestors is worthy of attention. Yiddish is older than English, originating in Spain in the thirteenth century and then becoming a more commonplace lingo after the fifteenth century when Jews migrated to Eastern Europe, Poland, Galicia, Hungary, Romania, and Russia. Yiddish comes from the German word *Judisch*, or Jewish. In the Yiddish language itself, Yiddish means Jewish.

Early on, Jewish mothers spoke the special tongue to their children at home, commanding attention like no other words to this day are able. For example, when my kids complain that they're bored, I respond unsympathetically with *"Klop der kop in der vant,"* which means "Beat your head against the wall." Need I say more?

Yiddish is not reserved for God's chosen people, although Jews seem to instinctively know how to make the *"cccchhh"* sound, similar to a fish bone stuck in their throat. Try saying *chutzpah*, *chuppa*, *challa*, or even *tuchas* without scratching your throat. It can't be done. And don't get me started on all the different ways to spell Yiddish words, such as *Hanuka*, *Chanukah*, *Hanukkah*, or *Channukah*, to name a few variations. The rules of Yiddish are as unique as brisket recipes.

One of my personal favorites, *mishegas*, which means craziness, also comes in *mishegoss* and *mishegaas*, unless referring to *meshugge*, which has the male counterpart *meshuggener* and the female *meshuggeneh*. It's all crazy to me.

To be fair, it's perfectly acceptable for millions of gentile Joe Schmoes to borrow Yiddish oldies-but-goodies like *oy*, even when their well-meaning intonations are awkward. By the way, *oy* is not even a word, but a vocabulary with 29 distinct variations, such as "*Oy vay!*" which means "Oh pain."

Other Yiddish influences on English words include *schmooze,* *schlimazel,* and *schlep.* In fact, research suggests that 500 Yiddish words appear in *Webster's Unabridged Dictionary,* but who's counting?

Another example is the Yiddish-American hopscotch chant that opened the classic American television show, *Laverne and Shirley.* Remember this? "Schlemiel! Schlimazel! Hasenpfeffer Incorporated!" Everyone sang the catchy theme song even if they didn't know what it meant.

The truth is, no other language eloquently conveys one's culture and religion with such sentiment, sarcasm, and wit. In my opinion, to lose the artful dialogue of Yiddish would be a disgrace to Judaism.

So, spread the word. Yiddish is coming!

Chapter 3
Lessons From The Sages

Teaching Children To Swim Gives Them Wings To Fly

If a typical Jewish mother is notorious for one thing, besides the curious habit of discussing dinner plans at lunchtime, it's the genetic disposition to love her children too much. I realize there are exceptions to this rule, but I'm not one of them. I spoil my kids, not so much with material things, but in a maternal way. In fact, I was the neurotic parent in playgroup who carried an apple corer and peeler in my diaper bag so that my infant son could nibble on a fresh, wholesome snack at the park.

Even now, I rarely leave the house without packing a "little something" in case Jack or Sari gets a hunger pang. When I take the kids to the swimming pool for lessons, for example, my oversized turquoise tote bag is so weighed down with bottled water, granola bars, cantaloupe balls, and spare change that I have no room for sunscreen. When the *Talmud* says "A father is obligated to teach his child to swim," I don't think toting snacks was what the Jewish thinkers had in mind.

In Judaism, "swim" refers to the skills and confidence a child needs to ride the waves in life. It's the greatest gift a parent can give a child, and it's also the hardest holy obligation of all. The lessons begin about the same time a mother squeezes inflatable water wings on the slippery, chubby arms of her baby. In Judaism, these wings to "swim" are eventually the wings to fly into adulthood. The sages had the foresight to know that if we continue to baby our children as they get older, we may deny them the valuable lessons that come when they make mistakes and get hurt.

For me, it starts with giving up some control over the little everyday things. In fact, I'm tested every morning when I painfully watch my fifth grader cram his feet into the back of his loosely laced Nikes without untying them first. I worry that if I don't double knot his tennis shoes, he might trip in gym class. That's when I quickly remind myself that if he stumbles on the track, I know he will pick himself up, dust himself off, and hopefully take the time to tie his shoes better the next day.

The same willpower to let go doesn't apply, however, when I obsessively clean my son's dirty eyeglasses. Even though Jack carries extra wipes in his batting bag, I still can't resist the temptation to sneak into the dugout around the fourth inning and make sure that he can see well enough out of his glasses to throw a change up. I realize that if I continue my inappropriate behavior when he pitches in the big leagues, I could be arrested.

Likewise, I try to let Sari learn from her mistakes, too. The other day, after her daddy warned her to not run in her flip-flops, she chased a ball across the street anyway and banged up her knee. As I bandaged her boo-boo and wiped away the flood of tears, she promised that she never would run in those shoes again. Also, I try not to resolve her conflicts every time she complains about a teacher at school or a friend in the neighborhood. I can't fix all of her problems. So most of the time, I just listen to her. She has to learn how to deal with all kinds of people, however unfair it may seem.

Even after I teach my children to "swim," I'll never stop worrying about them. So as summer approaches, I better dig my beach bag out of the closet and stock up on trail mix and tough love.

The Holiness Of Chores Makes A Perfect Boredom Buster

Nothing sends chills up my spine more than when my kids whine, "I'm borrrrred." How is boredom possible when our three-car garage is so jam-packed with bikes, scooters, skates, and every size and type of ball imaginable that I can barely squeeze my minivan into it? Never mind the pogo stick, jump ropes, sidewalk chalk, bubbles, water balloons, and countless Frisbees that I can't seem to get rid of. If the temperature is above freezing, I usually push them out the door and order them to "Go play!"

When my kids venture back indoors for something to do, they can watch TV and play computer games, but I usually steer them toward a dizzying array of other activities: books, music, art, games, puzzles, trading cards, a chalk board, ping pong table, punching bag, hoola-hoops, millions of Lego pieces, and assorted musical instruments that include a hand-me-down piano to bang out *Heart and Soul*.

So with all these things to do, why are my kids still bored? First of all, boredom is not a problem that needs to be fixed. My children eventually will discover that life is not about constant external stimulation. In fact, Judaism values these empty times to discover something about ourselves. Sometimes this lesson is a little easier with very young children, who are usually content to play with cardboard boxes, masking tape, and empty paper towel tubes. Judaism reminds us that ordinary things like cardboard rocket ships give our children the potential to reach for the stars, and therein lies the core of our religion.

When it comes to boredom, our Jewish ancestors had yet another answer: *"Klop der kop in der vant,"* one of my favorite Yiddish expressions that translates to "Go bang your head against the wall!" I love this phrase so much because it sums up my frustration. In fact, I want to frame the message and hang it in my kitchen, but I don't know how to needlepoint or do calligraphy.

My husband's Grandma Ruth taught me this timeless sentiment because her mother Minnie used to say it to her when she complained about having nothing to do. Back in those days, Great Grandma Minnie was too busy to entertain her three children, who grew up walking distance from the downtown *shul.* Instead, the Lithuanian immigrant baked bread and poked coals in the furnace at the crack of dawn so that her family would wake up to a warm house and breakfast on the table. As a schoolgirl, it was Grandma Ruth's job to wash the back steps on her hands and knees every Thursday afternoon.

Life is simpler now, or is it? Washing machines may take the place of washboards, but the idea of everyone pitching in around the house has become a job left undone. Let's face it, our kids are lazier than the generations before them, and it's our fault. The rabbis from long ago had a solution: chores. The whole idea is that a child who helps out around the house at an early age eventually will contribute to the community. A child who works as a team to make the home run smoother will grow up to serve others and value the tradition of *mitzvot,* ritual or ethical obligation. Way before parenting experts came along, these highly intelligent thinkers made a connection between chores and holiness—brilliant!

Judaism builds chores into the religion without being obvious. On Friday nights, for example, everyone can do his or her part for Shabbat, whether the job is to light candles or sprinkle sesame seeds on home baked challah. On holidays such as Hanukkah, it's a tradition for Sari to sprinkle blue sugar on dreidel cookies and for Jack to use toothpicks to dig wax out of the menorah.

Chores don't have to be fun, and they don't have to be done perfectly. As long as the job is practical for the age of the child, the lesson of responsibility hopefully will come across. For example, Jack is mature enough to walk our dog and Sari, a consummate picker-upper, folds towels and underwear better than I do. If each small act is part of a larger effort to honor God, then taking out the trash is not really a dirty job after all.

While it sometimes feels like my kids have less time to be kids because of their busy schedules, I don't feel guilty about giving them chores. They may not realize it now, but I'm doing them a favor. Eventually, I want them to move out of the house and be independent, self-reliant adults, right? Absolutely, as long as they call me everyday and let me do their laundry when they come over for dinner.

Being Jewish Means Dressing The Part

As I struggle everyday to pick my battles with my children, I usually surrender in the wardrobe war. In fact, for the most part, I let Jack and Sari wear what they want. Jack's usual attire consists of a Hanes undershirt and athletic shorts. When he dresses formal, he hangs a shark's tooth around his neck. Sari grabs the same striped pink tank top and ruffled skirt every time. Whenever I suggest that she wear something different, she looks at me like I'm as outdated as a taffeta prom gown.

With kids, clothing is all about control and self-expression. Jack never even notices the short-sleeved plaid shirt that hangs on his bedroom doorknob all summer long. A true baseball fan, he'd rather sport his favorite Ozzie Smith Cardinals jersey. Sari has a mind of her own as well. Whatever ensemble I suggest, she picks an entirely different outfit. I say bolero jacket; she says hooded sweater. In most cases, clothes are not worth fighting about.

But clothes are important and the High Holidays are the perfect time to teach our children how clothes can make the man, literally. In the Torah, many verses are devoted to the subject of *Bigdei Kodesh*, which is the holy clothing or ritual garments for the high priests. In the bible, Moses is told, "Make *Bigdei Kodesh*– holy garments–for Aaron your brother, for dignity and splendor." The text goes on to describe how the robe is made of "turquoise wool...pomegranates of blue, purple and scarlet yarns...twisted and finely woven linen...bells of pure gold...with the inscription: Holy to the Lord."

Judaism teaches us a couple of lessons here: inner beauty and how we treat others is what matters most. However, outward beauty is also symbolic when our apparel is used for a holy purpose. When we pray at temple, that's a holy purpose. Plus, the clothing we wear influences how we feel about ourselves and how others see us, just as it did for the high priest Aaron.

I'm not asking Sari to squeeze into tights unless for some reason she wants to torture herself during the sermon. And I'm not asking Jack to put on a suit and tie. In fact, the only criterion that I enforce for Jack is that he remove his filthy Rams football cap that he worships like an heirloom *yarmulke*. All I ask is that at synagogue my children dress a little differently than they normally would if they were at Busch Stadium. Sure I want my kids to feel comfortable and be themselves, but at the same time, I want them to show some respect in our house of worship.

I understand why many reformed temples these days allow a casual dress code. A relaxed atmosphere encourages families with young children to walk in the door. A rabbi wants everyone to feel welcome no matter what. Even so, it won't keep many of us moms from buying a new outfit for the Jewish New Year.

Turn Your Dinner Table Into An Altar

When I was a child growing up in the 1970s and the television classic *Leave it to Beaver* was considered a reality show, one of my most vivid everyday family rituals was the dinner hour. The dinner was the same—on Mondays, broiled chicken sprinkled with nothing more than paprika, not even salt—and so was the hour—five o'clock when my dad walked in the back door from work and emptied his car keys onto the counter.

My mother followed the old-fashioned food pyramid like it was one of the Ten Commandments: A mother shall serve her children a protein (preferably dried out), two vegetables, one starch, a glass of cold low-fat milk, and, on special occasions, lime gelatin with sliced bananas for dessert.

Although we were all well-nourished back then, today our family is grateful to reap the benefits of my mom's greatly improved culinary skills that include the best-ever matzo ball soup, cranberry chicken, kasha and shells, broccoli casserole, and perfectly shaped, baked from scratch chocolate chip cookies.

Even though I make some of my mom's wonderful recipes and follow the Food Network like some people tune into *American Idol*, the traditional dinner hour remains elusive to me. Like most modern families with busy lifestyles and demanding schedules, our plate is so full of after-school activities that it seems impossible sometimes to serve everyone a wholesome meal that doesn't include Honey Nut Cheerios for an appetizer.

For example, at least once a week, Jack dunks his last chicken finger in ketchup and darts off to batting practice before I even have a chance to fill my water glass. Jewish thinkers over the centuries give us some tasty advice on this common domestic dilemma. Ever since the destruction of the ancient holy temple, the sages tell us "every table in every home has become an altar." In other words, the dining table belongs to us and to God and therefore should be a place to nourish our body, mind, and soul in a peaceful setting.

Furthermore, Judaism teaches us that the dinner table is a place where a family comes together to appreciate the blessings in our lives. In my house, the only one who truly appreciates my spaghetti and meatballs is my curly-haired pooch Luci, who always scratches my leg for a second helping. One way I try to set the pace for a more enjoyable meal is saying *Hamotsi*. This prayer reminds my children that their food comes from God, not just the grocery store. Plus, when we start with a blessing, my family's mood is more relaxed and offers the perfect opportunity for me to give them something to really chew on, like conversation.

On these special occasions, I try to reconnect with my children and encourage them to talk about their day in between my orders to use a fork, not talk with their mouths full, and to eat something green. Whenever possible, I ask each person at the table to share his or her favorite part of the day or what they are most proud of. On a recent night, the dinner dialogue went something like this:

Sari: "My favorite part of the day is when daddy comes home."
Jack: "I am proud that I studied really hard for my science test and got an A and that I beat the toughest fifth grader in tetherball."
Scott: "My favorite part is when I come home and my kids run into my arms."
Me: "My favorite part is right now, eating this apple raisin koogle."

Long before Weight Watchers came along, the Talmud

recommends that we eat slowly and chew our food well, which helps control overeating. Even though the rabbis place great value on the manner in which we eat our meals, I still can't help myself when I stand at the kitchen counter and pick the crispy noodles off the top of the casserole.

Food For Thought

With the kitchen as my laboratory, I like to experiment on my husband and children with new recipes that I want to try out before I serve anything to a "real" guest. No matter how many times I attempt to make marinated flank steak, the meat is never edible and usually too tough to chew. On the other hand, whenever I get lucky and concoct something particularly tasty, such as a new twist on corn flake chicken, I can't seem to duplicate the meal the same way again. This drives my taste testers crazy.

I have other tricks up my apron as well. My son Jack, a very picky eater, often prefers the school cafeteria food to my own cooking. So when I bake something like three-cheese lasagna, I tell him that I got the recipe from the Rockwood School District. That way, he at least tries the cheesy noodles before he trades in his plate for another peanut butter tortilla.

I find that my altar, the kitchen table, is also a great place to wet my family's appetite for something other than tuna noodle casserole. In fact, my goal is to feed their hunger for knowledge whenever possible, or at least get my kids to think about something more significant than downloading songs on iTunes.

I had the perfect opportunity to serve some food for thought the other day. As I read my parenting bible, Wendy Mogel's *The Blessing of a Skinned Knee*, I learned about a common question that rabbis ask their students, "What is the most important moment in Jewish history?" Hint: It's kind of a trick question, but the answer is so simple. I can't wait to give my family the same test.

To reward my family in advance for their participation, I toss another handful of seasoned croutons in the salad. Anything crunchy seems to always lift everyone's spirits. Here goes the conversation:

Me: "I have an interesting question that I want you to give some thought, and then tell me your honest answer while we sit here together and enjoy this delicious mostaccioli."
Jack: "Uh oh. Mom must be writing another story because she's getting weird again."
Me: "The question is: What is the most important moment in Jewish history?"

Everyone stops chewing for a while and digests what I just asked them. Finally, my son offers the first guess.

Jack: "The most important moment in Jewish history is when Israel became a state."
Sari: "When the Jewish people got Shabbat."
Scott: "When God parted the Red Sea. Now pass the parmesan please."
Grandma Charlotte: "When God gave Moses the Ten Commandments."
Me: "According to the rabbi, the answer is: THIS is the most important moment in Jewish history."

At first, there's silence. Everyone looks confused. Then my daughter speaks up.

Sari: "I don't get it. How can having dinner right now be the most important moment in Jewish history?

Me: "The rabbi means that being together in this moment is all that counts right now. And that whatever happened yesterday or whatever activity is scheduled for tomorrow is not important today. Because all we have is this moment."

Sari: "What's for dessert?"

Angels, Devils, Best Friends

Stay-at-home-moms are much like corporate executives because we problem solve all day long. The only difference is that our boss is four-feet tall and considers Lunchables a gourmet meal. And another thing—no one recognizes our everyday accomplishments, big or small, such as the many times I salvage artwork from the bottom of a trash can after it's already soaked in cream of mushroom soup. Even though we don't get the same perks as businesspeople, moms are on a fast track with no plans to slow down anytime soon.

I always look for creative ways to solve problems. Sometimes I'm worthy of a promotion; other times I deserve to get fired. As a Jewish mom, one of the more challenging, long-term assignments on my agenda is to identify and understand my children's *yetzer tov*, or impulse for good, and *yetzer hara*, or impulse for evil. As I understand it, the *yetzer tov* is the angel that reminds us to follow God's law when we are tempted to do something forbidden. The *yetzer hara* is more like the devil that stops at nothing to satisfy our personal needs. It's not necessarily a bad thing, though. For example, it's the selfish desire of *yetzer hara* that leads us to get married, create babies, and advance in business, all of which makes the world go round.

The rabbis in the Talmud believe that God gives everyone at birth both a *yetzer tov* and *yetzer hara*. The Talmud notes that both impulses are essential to human survival. How we balance the two forces in our lives describes the essence of free will.

Especially in children, the *yetzer hara* gets the most attention, at least at my house, because it's the loudest and most demanding. For Jack, it's an intense mental and physical focus on the ball field that drives him to pitch another shutout inning. That's a good thing. His relentless *yetzer hara* also bullies him, and he can be way too hard on himself if he doesn't perform his personal best. That's a bad thing.

For Sari, her *yetzer hara* is the tenacity to question everything that doesn't seem right or fair, such as the grading scale that she helped revise in first grade. Any positive change is a good thing. However, the *yetzer hara* also makes it harder for her to go with the flow. Many times the *yetzer hara* gets stuck in the negative and shadows the bright side of a situation. And that's a bad thing.

When guided in the right direction, the rabbis tell us, the energy of the *yetzer hara* is what gives our child a one-of-a-kind spunk in his or her personality. It's the fire that burns inside our child and no parent has the right to extinguish it. The trick is to find our child's greatest strength hidden inside his or her worst quality. The first step is to look at ourselves in the mirror. Where do you think our child's *mishegas* comes from in the first place? Not a pretty sight.

A Penny For Your Complaints

If a child's greatest strength is indeed hidden inside his or her worst quality, as Jewish wisdom tells us about the *yetzer hara,* then I'm determined to find the value of my daughter Sari's *kvetvching.*

Like many little girls her age, Sari, at 7, has the tendency to complain about everything from the seams in her socks to the way I brush her hair. I try to be sensitive to her sensitivities and I respect the fact that she's very intuitive and mature for her age. However, Sari's persistent habit has become an art form in both English and Yiddish. For example:

"This cockamamy puzzle doesn't fit together!"
"I'm tired of *schlepping* in the van. I want to go home!"
"This *schmata* has a stain and I'm not wearing it!"

I realize that in order for parents to change their child's behavior, they must first look at themselves in the mirror. In this case, Sari gets her feisty attitude partially from her father, who is known to say things like this in front of his impressionable offspring:

"That new restaurant will never make it—the food is garbage and the owner is a *gonef*."

"The driver in front of me is moving like an *alter kocker*. Get goin' already!"

"Stop *hockin'* me. I'll be ready in a minute."

"Why can't anyone design a decent vacuum? This piece of *hazarai* just pushes dirt around."

I know, what am I complaining about? At least my husband vacuums.

So in order to reduce the number of negative statements in my household, I invented a fun game called the "complaint container." I introduce my suggestion one lazy Sunday morning during a pillow fight in our king-size bed.

"Hey everyone, I want to call a family meeting about something that has been on my mind for quite awhile," I start out, trying to dodge an oversized feather pillow that smacks my face. "All of us like to complain about stuff, so starting today, I want everyone to put a penny in a pot for every gripe he or she makes and see how many coins we collect at the end of the day. The complaint container is not meant as a punishment, but as a learning experience for all of us."

To break the silence, which is their reaction to my idea, I quickly add, "Besides, we can use the money we collect to do something fun together as a family."

Finally, I hear a voice from under the sea of sheets. "It takes a lot of pennies to amount to anything," mumbles Jack, who is not so much a vocal complainer as a door slammer. "What are we going to do with all the money we collect—split a pack of gum?" My son has a point. I can't even buy a postage stamp with say, 27 cents. Even though that's a lot of complaints, it's not a lot of change. I realize that I have some kinks to work out, but it's a start. "Okay, let's make it a nickel, or a dime," I suggest.

Jack leans on an elbow and counters my offer. "How about $5 for every complaint?"

With that remark, Sari crawls her way out and says, "This silly game makes no sense, and I'm not playing! Besides, how can we start when we don't even have a pot or container or whatever you call it," she adds, wrapping her arms tighter around her father, who pretends to sleep.

I realize that I must jump on this project quickly before the momentum disappears. At least I have everyone's attention. Immediately, I begin to take mental notes on complaints throughout the day.

"Chicken stir fry again? Disgusting!" Ka-ching.

"I can't concentrate on my computer game when my sister is

bothering me." Ka-ching.

"This-boy-in-my-class-was-picking-his-nose-and-spreading-germs-and-I-better-not-get-sick-because-then-I-would-miss-my-soccer-game-and-I-would-be-sooooooo-mad…" Ka-ching, ka-ching, ka-ching!

I feverishly dig through my mismatched Tupperware and come up with an empty 32-ounce yogurt container. I attack this craft like an overzealous preschooler. I cover the container with whatever construction paper I find in the closet. I decorate the lid and cut a slit for the coins. To make it official, I try to come up with a creative name, like "Pouty Pot" or something cutesy. Instead, I simply label the can: COMPLAINTS HERE. 1 CENT.

I gleam with pride at the finished product—not bad for a mom who accidentally cut two holes for the head of her daughter's first Halloween ghost costume. When Sari later asks me for change for a nickel out of the decorated yogurt container, I question where this game is headed. At least we can laugh about it. And that beats complaining for now.

My Kids Teach Me

As parents, we are our children's first teachers. Never mind the fact that I haven't understood my son's math homework since he was in third grade. But when it comes to life lessons, such as teaching the value of helping others, Judaism takes our responsibility as good role models very seriously. In fact, the Hebrew word for parents, *horim*, shares the same root word *morim*, which means teacher.

Still, I have to admit that the roles are often reversed in my home and my kids are the teachers who show me what's really important. I just have to keep my eyes and ears open at all times. When

Sari described the white foamy bubbles in her bath as "fluffy as grandma's sponge cake," she unknowingly reminded me that I should use more metaphors in my writing.

My kids always make me stop and think, whether I'm in the mood to or not. When Sari asks me how many days she has been alive, it's not good enough to make a guess. I go for the calculator. On a spiritual level, she challenges me to question the goodness of God when evil things happen in our world. These days, she is hung up on why God would send the 10 plagues and kill all those Egyptians and animals when they had done nothing wrong. If anything, she opens the door for discussions and makes me wonder how we hang onto our faith sometimes.

As Sari and Jack grow up, they continue to teach me in many different ways. For example, when Jack decided to donate the gifts that his friends gave him on his 11th birthday to a local charity, I first thought he was kidding. I mean, it wasn't even *Mitzvah* Day or an annual toy drive. After all, a birthday is that one special day all year that gives children an excuse to update their wish lists with all the stuff that they didn't get for Hanukkah. So when Jack wanted to share his abundance with others less fortunate, I wondered if he felt okay. I pondered to myself, what were the strings attached to this deal? By any chance, were the strings attached to a brand new electric guitar?

So I asked him, "Jack, are you sure you want to give away your presents that your friends bring you, even if one of the gifts is a really cool baseball card?" Without hesitation he answered, "Yep, I already have everything I need."

I experienced a parental epiphany at the moment I realized Jack truly wanted to make his birthday special not only for himself, but for other kids who might not have a closet full of brand new toys. Needless to say, I was so proud of my son. And like any good Jewish mother, I felt guilty. I was ashamed that I had doubted his heartfelt desire to help other people. His generosity taught me that any lifecycle event, such as a birthday, anniversary, new baby, or in the memory of a loved one, is an opportunity to partner with God to help "repair the world," or *tikkun olam*.

After Jack's birthday, when my kids and I delivered bags of Nerf footballs and Legos to the residents at HavenHouse, we didn't realize we had fulfilled the *mitzvah bikkur holim*, which means to visit and help the sick. We didn't think about *tzedakah* when we helped bring smiles to children and their families who came there from all over the country to benefit from advanced medical care in our community. All we knew was that it felt right, and it was a lesson worth repeating.

Sukkot **Transforms Your Backyard Into A** *Bimah*

During the Hebrew month of *Tishrei*, Jews go from the most solemn day of the year, Yom Kippur, to one of the simplest, *Sukkot*, which celebrates the plentiful fall harvest. In a period of just 14 days, we move from the glorified High Holidays to the most down-to-earth festival of all. In the time it takes to polish off the last bite of leftover brisket, we transcend from praying in the majestic, stained-glass surroundings in our congregation to shaking the *lulav* with our children in a makeshift outdoor hut. The synagogue is heavenly. The *sukkah*, literally, is under the heavens. Only in Judaism can we call both the *bimah* and our backyard a sacred place.

Sukkot, a Hebrew word that means "booths," is the commemoration of the 40 years our ancestors wandered in the Sinai Desert and set up these temporary shelters. When we invite a guest, called *ushpizin*, to join us in our *sukkah* for a meal, we symbolically recall the commandment to dwell in booths for seven days. Spending time together under the stars not only reminds Jews of their roots to the land, but also teaches an important Jewish philosophy to live in balance.

Rabbis reinforce this profound concept when they tell the story about how to keep two pieces of paper in our pockets at all times. On one piece, we write, "I am a speck of dust." On the other, we write, "The world was created for me."

With these words, we realize that we are nothing. And we are everything. When we gaze up to the sparkly heavens on a chilly autumn night, the *sukkah* reminds us how significant, and yet how small, we really are in the scheme of things. We have a place in the world and we are connected to a greater being. At the same time, our problems are so trivial.

When we spend time outdoors in a *sukkah*, we feel that God through nature is part of our everyday lives. We recognize God's role when we gather the four species of the festive holiday bouquet called the

Cousins decorate our backyard *sukkah*, October 2009.

lulav. The *lulav* is made of three leafy branches—the tall palm tree branch, willow twigs, and myrtle leaves—which are bound together with braided palm leaves.

Although it's a *mitzvah* to gather the four species ourselves, we also can conveniently buy a *lulav*, as well as a *sukkah* kit, at many area temples. The ritual is to hold the *lulav* in our right hand and the *etrog,* which looks like a big lemon and has a sweet smell, in our left. Then, we wave the *lulav* in all directions (east, south, west, north, up and down) to show that God's goodness is everywhere. We say the *Sukkot* blessing: "Praised are You, Adonai our God, Ruler of the world, who makes us holy with *mitzvot* and commands us to dwell in the *sukkah*."

By the way, you don't have to be a carpenter to build a *sukkah*. In fact, there are very few rules to follow, so let your family's imagination go wild.

Rule #1: A *sukkah* has to have at least three walls. You can start with the side of your house for one of the walls. To make the job easier, my family uses another shortcut—an already existing garden gazebo on the patio. We have netting for the sides, but it can be constructed from any material, such as lattice, old doors, plywood, sheets, canvas, waterproof tarp, anything that can withstand the wind.

Rule #2: The roof has to be see through and preferably made from a natural earth product, such as branches, corn stalks, bamboo reeds, or sticks that give shade and allow those inside to see the evening stars in the sky.

Rule #3: Encourage all generations in your family to help decorate the *sukkah* and have fun! We trim our spiritual structure with pumpkins, corn stalks, colorful mums, sunflowers, fruit and acorn chains, Indian corn, Rosh Hashanah cards, Jewish artwork, and whatever else reminds us of the bountiful autumn season.

Who knows, I might never want to eat at the kitchen table again.

Tu Bishvat **Plants Roots In Our World**

In the dead of winter, cherry blossoms bloom in Brooklyn, New York. And in the Midwest, the unseasonably mild weather allows

Jack to still wear gym shorts when he plays basketball in the driveway. One day it's 80 degrees; the next day it's 40.

Seems innocent enough, but truthfully I wonder if this bizarre temperature pattern is a subtle warning sign that our environment is in trouble. After watching former vice president Al Gore's global warming documentary, *An Inconvenient Truth*, which explores the effects of arctic melt rates, devastating heat waves, and dangerous changes in ocean currents, I'm convinced that our children's future is at risk if we don't clean up our act, literally.

Scientific buzzwords, like global warming, climate change, and greenhouse effect are no longer limited to a political agenda but determine our survival. Since the beginning, Judaism has taught us to appreciate and take care of the intricate ecosystem that God has given us. Just recently the rest of the world has started listening.

Tu Bishvat, or Jewish Earth Day, is the time to educate ourselves about the interdependence between trees and human and animal life. We require oxygen and produce carbon dioxide; trees and other plants require carbon dioxide and produce oxygen. When we destroy forested land, we lose forms of life. No wonder the Torah is called "a tree of life for them that hold fast to it." It's our job as parents to plant the seeds of knowledge when it comes to environmentally friendly habits.

So what can we do today to improve our world tomorrow? According to the National Resources Defense Council, if we all recycle our Sunday newspapers we could save more than 500,000 trees *every week*. There's a lot more we can do, too, including recycle everything from newspapers and magazines to plastic containers and motor oil and many more common household items that are listed in the book *50 Simple Things You Can Do To*

Save The Earth. For example:

• Remind your children to turn off the lights and computer when they leave a room. According to the World Resources Institute, the more electricity we use the more industrial emissions we generate, contributing heavily to problems like the greenhouse effect and acid rain.

• Share a ride and carpool to soccer games and other activities. If each commuter car carries just one more person, we'd save 600,000 gallons of gasoline a day and prevent 12 million pounds of carbon dioxide from polluting the atmosphere.

• Styrofoam, which is actually polystyrene foam and made from a known carcinogen, benzene, is completely non-biodegradable and wastes already limited space in landfills. Even 500 years from now, that foam cup that held your cappuccino this morning might still sit on the Earth's surface. Even worse, it can float in the water and kill marine life.

• Get a grip on faucets and turn off tap water while you brush teeth, shave, and wash dishes. A household can save up to 20,000 gallons of water each year by doing so.

• Instead of plastic or paper grocery bags, re-use canvas tote bags when you shop. It takes one 15- to 20-year old tree to make enough paper for only 700 grocery bags. Plastic bags aren't degradable and are made from petroleum, a nonrenewable resource. Plus, plastic bags wind up in the ocean and kill marine animals because they get tangled up in the trash bags and swallow them.

• Last, but not least, plant trees, which has been the major custom of *Tu Bishvat* for thousands of years. Americans use 50 million tons of paper annually, which means that we consume more than 850 million trees.

As we become more aware of our global environmental problems, *Tu Bishvat* has evolved from merely a marker on the calendar to a national celebration of our Jewish heritage and the preservation of our natural resources. By the way, the name *Tu Bishvat* is the Hebrew abbreviation of *tet* and *vav*, which adds up to fifteen. So *Tu Bishvat* literally means "the fifteenth of the Hebrew month of *Shevat*."

Also known as the "birthday of the trees," *Tu Bishvat* is first mentioned in the *Mishnah*, where the rabbis explain to ancient farmers that *Tu Bishvat* is the New Year for trees, just as Rosh Hashanah is the New Year for people. The date makes perfect sense because the majority of the annual rainfall in Israel typically occurs after mid-winter (usually in February) when the saturated soil is just ripe for planting new trees.

At home, your family can plant a tree at a local park, school, or in your own yard when the ground is ready. If you don't have a green thumb and aren't sure how to get started, call or visit a local nursery or horticultural society. Meanwhile, you can grow parsley indoors in preparation for your Passover seder.

No Jewish holiday is complete without a feast. So throw a fruit party or host a *Tu Bishvat seder* with delicacies reminiscent of Israel.

Chapter 4
It's All About The Food

Passover Brings Out The Child In All Of Us

Passover is one of the most memorable holidays of the Jewish calendar and not just because we eat matzo for seven days straight. Growing up, everyone has different memories of the seder, depending on how many hours it takes to retell the story of how our courageous ancestor Israelites journeyed from slavery to freedom. What I remember most about my childhood seders is everyone being together and that our rituals seemed long enough for the wilted parsley to look appetizing. The grownups read prayers while my brother Steve and I tried to keep our hands to ourselves. The only thing that kept my bobbing head from landing on Grandma Ida's Lenox china was the anticipation of finding the hidden piece of matzo wrapped in a linen napkin. If I were lucky, I might win one of Grandpa Harry's shiny silver dollars.

While Passover is rich in tradition, from the *Haggadah* to the farfel koogle, the experiences and lessons learned are brand new each year. In fact, ever since Jack and Sari were old enough to pronounce the word *afikoman*, I was determined to liven up the seder and feed their imaginations as well as their bellies. Fortunately, most temples and Jewish preschools offer a gold mine of resources that give families creative ideas on how to make your seder more fun and meaningful for everyone.

I go a little crazy on Passover. And the best part? I don't have to cook and clean. Usually, Uncle Keith and Aunt Amy host the first night and our family friends "Uncle Barry" and "Aunt Ilene" graciously open their home to us on the second night for an encore performance. All I have to do is show up with a triple batch of *charoset* and a huge plastic storage box filled with surprises. Preparation is key to a smooth seder, so I make sure I bring plenty of crayons and paper placemats for the little ones to color. After that, I pull out stickers to decorate Elijah's plastic wine cup. When it's time for the older cousins to read the Four Questions, they pass around oversized, colored index cards that I laminated to prevent grape juice stains. I'm a little *meshugee* this time of year, what can I say?

The first night of Passover truly is different from all other nights. Why? Among other things, the youngsters get to stay up late on a school night, eat more junk food than usual, have permission to croak like frogs, and don't even have to sit up straight at the table. In fact, my kids bring a fluffy pillow with them to recline at the seder. The pillow is special because we painted candlesticks and *Kiddush* cups on the pillowcase, and we use it only on this holiday.

Perhaps the most entertaining part of the evening—besides Uncle Keith's jokes about the rabbi, the priest, and the Buddhist—is when the kids act out the 10 plagues. Each participant gets a bag filled with props that represent each terrible punishment given to the Egyptians for their mistreatment of Jews. In our family, for example, rubber frogs and silly sunglasses (for the three days of darkness) are as much a tradition as matzo balls and gefilte fish. I actually encourage the children to throw plastic golf balls at each other to symbolize a hailstorm. Even the adults get a kick out of pouring water into a pitcher that magically turns into blood with a few drops of food coloring.

Finding the *afikoman* is another highlight, only nowadays every child gets a prize so that no one's self-esteem is hurt. While some traditions change, others stay the same. Either way, our children will always remember being together.

Here's my favorite recipe for *charoset*, which I have revised over the years with more Mogan David wine as my kids get older. This is a tripled recipe, keeping in mind that my side of the family used to eat the sweet mixture (that symbolizes the clay used to build pyramids) as a main dish.

Ellie's Charoset

8 large tart apples, unpeeled, cored, and grated
4 c. pecans or walnuts, finely chopped
8 T. honey
4 t. cinnamon
1 ½ c. blackberry or grape kosher wine

Mix grated apples and chopped nuts together in a big bowl. Add rest of ingredients and mix well. Chill. To add a little variety to your seder, try other variations of *charoset*, like using raisins and dates instead of apples.

Curiosity Keeps Seder Alive

You know how little kids ask their parents "why" all the time? Everything is a question. Why is the sky blue? Why do I sleep with my eyes closed? Why is applesauce mushy? Why is your name mommy? When we give them an answer, they usually follow up with another "why" all over again. This unending conversation can drive a parent crazy.

In Judaism, the curious child in all of us keeps our religion alive. This lesson is never clearer than at Passover. In fact, when it comes to the Passover seder, the question "why" is the focus of the entire service, and the answers are found in the *Haggadah*, which means "retelling the story."

The ancient rabbis who created the symbolic Passover seder were nothing short of brilliant. Step by step, from making a Hillel sandwich of "bricks-and-mortar" to opening the door for Elijah, the sages ingeniously constructed a participatory service that caters specifically to the next generation of Jews. After a few blessings, the festive meal kicks up a notch with the Four Questions, called the *Mah Nishtanah*, and the rest of the ceremony heats up from there. The rituals are designed to stimulate all the senses so that even the grape juice drinkers can stay awake long enough to see if the prophet ever shows up. Just when you think the party is over and you're stuffed with matzo balls and macaroons, it's time for the wound-up kids to scramble for the *afikomen* and win a prize. From beginning to end, the Passover seder is a masterpiece of pedagogy.

Most children learn by doing, and there's plenty to do at the Passover seder, from acting out the 10 plagues to singing the *Dayenu* and lots of eating in between. For the visual learners, the seder plate alone tells the whole story of our Exodus from Egypt more than 3,000 years ago. The shankbone, for example, explains how the Hebrews sacrificed a lamb to God in gratitude for "passing over" their first-born child. The *maror*, or bitter herbs, shows the bitterness that our ancestors experienced as slaves. The *karpas*, or parsley, symbolizes spring and the spirit of hope for our future. A roasted egg tells of the continuing cycle of life, as well as the festival offering brought to the Temple in Jerusalem in ancient times. The sticky *charoset* depicts the mortar that our forefathers used to make bricks in Egypt. A dish of salt water illustrates the tears that we shed when we were slaves in Egypt.

When the youngest child proudly asks, "Why is this night different than all other nights?" everyone at the table is encouraged to play a role in answering him. For the one and only time of the year, probably, the youngster has everyone's undivided attention. By tradition, the stimulating parent-child dialogue begins:

"On all other nights we eat either *chametz* (leavened bread) or matzo, but tonight we only eat matzo. Why?"
"On all other nights we eat any vegetables, bitter or not bitter, but tonight we only eat *marror*. Why?"
"On all other nights we do not have to dip our food even once, but tonight we dip twice—once *karpas* in salt water and once *marror* in *charoset*. Why?"
"On all other nights we sit either straight or leaning, but tonight we all lean on pillows instead of sitting up straight in our chairs. Why?"

Now that's a mouth full! Fortunately, the *Haggadah* provides all the clever, visual guidelines parents need to teach their children about how their Jewish history influences who they are today.

In Deuteronomy it says, "And thou shall tell thy son on that day, saying, 'This is what the Lord did to US when WE came out of Egypt.'"

Besides, it's not so much the questions that are important, but the act of asking that is the greater lesson. In short, the CliffsNotes answer is: We eat matzo and *marror* to remind us of when we were slaves; we eat *charoset* and recline on pillows to remind us of our freedom. The miracle of the story is that we were slaves, but "*Hashem* (the God of our ancestors)...took us out." We were slaves and kings on the same night, and that's why we celebrate Passover.

Moreover, the *Haggadah* is way ahead of its time when it comes to educational parenting advice as explained in the *midrash* of the four children (wise, wicked, simple, young), which exists in all of us. According to the Torah, it's a *mitzvah*, a commandment, for parents to explain the meaning of Passover and Exodus in a way that every type of child can understand.

For example, the wise child wants to learn. When this one asks, "What are the testimonies, the statutes, and the laws which the Lord your God has commanded you?" you should teach him "all the laws from the *Mishna* up to the last law of the seder, which is that we are not allowed to eat after the *Afikoman*."

When the wicked child asks, "Why do you go to the trouble of doing this service?" he thinks that the *mitzvahs* are only for the other person and not for himself. Even when the evil one doesn't believe in the Torah, he is still accepted in the Jewish family because he is a Jew. Explain to him, "It was because of the *mitzvahs* that *Hashem* did miracles for ME (and not for people like him) when I left Egypt."

When the simple child asks, "What is this all about?" say to him, "We do these *mitzvahs* because *Hashem* used his strong hand to save us from slavery in Egypt."

For the child who doesn't even understand enough to ask, you must start at the beginning of the Passover story.

For the child in all us, the Passover celebration is the best way to learn about our Jewish past, present, and future.

Lots Of Matzo Tempts The Taste Buds

Welcome to Passover, a seven-day matzo festival in which Jews everywhere remember their history of slavery and celebrate their freedom by concocting appetizing ways to eat plain crackers for an entire week. And like every other symbolic Jewish food, matzo has a dramatic story behind it.

Matzo, which is referred to as *lechem oni*, or the "bread of affliction," represents the hardships that our ancestors faced in fighting Egyptian slavery. In the story of Exodus, the Israelites escaped their bondage in Egypt and hurriedly fled in the middle of the night before the dough had a chance to rise. On their way to the Promised Land of Canaan, the Jews took the dough with them and baked the flat, hard cakes, called matzo, in the hot dessert sun. This simple unleavened bread has a message: we must hurry today to help all those who are not free.

Matzo, which is made of only flour and water, has pretty much remained the same over the centuries. Aside from a satisfying crunch, matzo is basically flavorless unless spread with butter, jelly, cheese, or your favorite "kosher for Passover" topping. But with a little imagination, matzo can be a tasty treat.

My favorite way to eat matzo is like a crispy pancake. First, I wet a sheet of matzo with water. Second, I beat an egg in a bowl and break the matzo into the bowl and coat it with egg. Third, I shape the crumbled matzo into a patty. Then, I fry the matzo in oil until golden brown. Now for the good part—I dip the pancake in honey and pop it in my mouth like I did when I was a kid.

Here are a few other tasty recipes. Matzo never tasted so sweet.

Chocolate Matzo Bark

Matzo – three or four sheets
1 c. butter
1 c. brown sugar
12 oz. semi-sweet chocolate chips
1 c. almonds (optional)

Preheat oven to 350 degrees. Use a cookie sheet with sides. Line with foil and spray with non-stick cooking spray. Cover entire surface with a single layer of matzo, breaking into pieces if necessary. In medium saucepan over high heat, bring butter and brown sugar to a boil. Lower heat to medium high and continue to simmer three minutes, stirring constantly. Pour this caramel over matzo. Bake for about five minutes, or until deep golden brown. Remove from oven. Sprinkle chocolate chips on top of caramel and let sit a few minutes. Swirl chocolate and top with nuts. Freeze or refrigerate until topping hardens. Break into small pieces and serve.

Passover Granola

4 c. matzo farfel
½ c. slivered almonds or walnuts
¾ c. shredded coconut
½ c. honey
½ c. vegetable oil
1 c. raisins

Preheat oven to 350 degrees. Mix farfel, nuts, and coconut in a bowl. Add honey and oil and mix well. Spread mixture in a single layer on non-stick baking sheets. Bake 20-30 minutes, stirring often to prevent burning. Remove from oven and add raisins. Mix well. Cool and store in an airtight container. Enjoy as a breakfast cereal with milk or a snack right out of the container.

The Torah, Like A Matzo Ball, Is A Never-Ending Circle

In the Hebrew month *Tishrei*, the season of renewal is not complete without the celebration of *Simchat Torah*, which means "Rejoicing the Torah." This celebration marks the completion of the annual cycle of weekly Torah portions, which is actually five books in one. The Five Books of Moses—Genesis, Exodus, Leviticus, Numbers, Deuteronomy—teach us how Moses received the Torah on Mount Sinai.

On *Simchat Torah*, we read the last Torah portion in Deuteronomy, then roll back to the Creation Story in Genesis, which reminds us that the Torah is a circle and never ends. On this holiday, Jews sing and dance around the synagogue with the Torah, while the children march and wave mini scrolls and flags. If ever God permits Jews to raise a toast and party hard like they've reached the Promised Land, *Simchat Torah* is the time.

In my perspective, the Torah is like a recipe book on how to live a good life. The ingredients include a mixture of fascinating stories about how the Jewish people began, our first fathers and mothers, and our escape from slavery in Egypt. Then we add the Ten Commandments and stir together a hearty portion of rules, laws, customs, and rituals.

Like the handwritten Torah pages, a recipe scrawled by your late great grandmother herself on a tattered and faded piece of paper is a historic document that will be lost if not delicately preserved and carefully handled. Both the Torah and Bubbeh's strudel recipe are handed down from generation to generation.

Like the lessons in the Torah, some teachings must always continue. For example, how to make the perfect matzo ball may not be in the Holy Scripture, but the tradition will never die in our family. When my mom told me the other day that she was thinking for the first time of buying matzo balls (a dollar a dumpling) at a nearby deli to heat with her homemade chicken soup, I had mixed emotions. I was relieved that she resolved not to slave as much in the kitchen in preparation for my brother and his wife's annual visit from Florida, but I was sad that the tradition of her matzo balls would come to an end. I felt that it was sacrilegious to serve a matzo ball at a family meal that was prepared by a stranger's hands.

So my husband Scott, who would much rather do the dishes than make any kind of dinner other than blueberry pancakes, came to the rescue and vowed to save his mother-in-law's homemade matzo ball from extinction. He solicited the help of his Grandma Ruth, who has made matzo balls from scratch for most of her 90 years, to come over and show him how it's done. I watched the whole family get into the act—Sari cracked the eggs on the rim of the bowl and let each one slide into the matzo meal mixture without one shell in the way. Jack stirred the melted butter, salt, and warm water into the batter. I admired how Scott wet his hands and proudly rolled the thick, sticky dough into the perfect size and dropped each one into boiling water.

Like scientists in a laboratory, Scott and his grandma watched the matzo balls pop to the top of the big pot on the stove. Finally, the experiment was a success, and I got to taste the matzo ball before it was introduced to my mom's rich, flavorful chicken soup with Kluski egg noodles and sweet, tender carrots. Needless to say, the matzo ball soup was scrumptious, maybe better than ever because of what it represents. Like the Torah, the matzo ball is a circle that never ends.

Invite Elijah With A Magical Cup

Each year at Passover, my goal is to learn something that I didn't know before and pass that new tradition on to my children so that they better understand their own heritage. In other words, I want them to appreciate who they are and where they've come from as Jews. After all, "Whoever expands on the Passover telling is to be praised," said the Jewish sages, and I need all the accolades that I can get.

Last year, for example, I tried out a new *Haggadah* called *The 30-Minute Seder,* which "blends brevity with tradition." It was a big hit because the vivid illustrations and simplified text were easy to follow yet thought provoking, right down to the explanation of the Hillel sandwich, or *Korech.* Actually, it was a toss up between *30-Minute Seder* and another child-friendly *Haggadah* that can be personalized with my name on the cover, such as, "Ellie's *Haggadah,*" and is available as a temple fundraiser through www.PersonalizedHagggadahs.com.

On this Festival of Freedom, I'll try anything, even the bitter herb if I'm hungry enough. One year, I asked everyone at the table to fill the wine cup of the person sitting next to them and taste what it's like to have their own servant during the multiple-course meal. Fortunately, I served white wine so that my sweater wasn't stained when Sari spilled kosher sauvignon blanc all over me. We also reclined on pillows and, needless to say, I was ready for a nap by the time we sang *Dayenu.*

After all, the Passover seder isn't just about telling the story of the Exodus, it's about experiencing the time when the Jews were slaves, so that's why I force my children to help me with the spring cleaning and remove all *chametz* from our home by candlelight and a feather duster.

When I was young, one of my favorite parts of the seder was

waiting for mysterious Elijah, the Hebrew prophet who opposed the worship of idols. The Hebrew name Eliyahu, by the way, means the Lord is my God, and according to tradition, Elijah came from a family of shepherds and lived in a cave on Mount Carmel in the ninth century B.C.E. during the reign of King Ahab and his wife, Queen Jezebel.

As a youngster during the seder, I would stare at the open door and wait for Elijah to come in and announce the Messiah and drink from the fifth cup of wine, or at least sip the matzo ball soup. It never happened, until this year.

A new cup that makes the wine disappear before everyone's eyes might sound a little corny, but it certainly grabs the attention of children and adults alike. In fact, not since I used red food coloring to make the waters of the Nile turn into blood as a demonstration of the first plague did a prank make a good point.

The magical contraption, which looks like a traditional wine-filled goblet with a beautiful engraving of a Star of David and the name *Eliyahu* in Hebrew, is called the "Elijah Drinks" cup and is the greatest thing since chocolate chip macaroons. This real conversation piece is the brainchild of Marc Jaffe, a comedy writer turned entrepreneur, who used to write for *Seinfeld* and *Mad About You*. Now Jaffe is making headlines with his seder schtick. Jaffe wanted to reenact the arrival of Elijah with a little more drama than shaking the dinner table. So he and his sidekick, fellow comedian and magician Kerry Pollock, came up with a plan. After nine months of testing and a lot of *brachah* (blessing) over each cup, the Elijah Drinks cup was born. Here's how it works:

The host of the seder lifts up the shiny sturdy aluminum cup to say the prayer and then sets it back down on the table, depressing a button at the bottom which slowly empties the wine into a secret compartment. Is that cool or what?

To see a demonstration of the Elijah Drinks cup on YouTube, visit Jaffe's website www.elijahdrinks.com. Jaffe also is working on prototypes for an *afikomin* detector and insta-fold *tallis*.

Apple Picking Ripens Awareness

An annual fall outing to the apple orchard is a fun way for families to kick off the Jewish New Year. The juicy apples are as crisp as the autumn air, and with each bite I taste the new season. Whenever I go apple picking I feel like a kid again. I also seem to lose my table manners. Where else can I gnaw on a piece of fruit and nonchalantly drop the core at my feet? Likewise, I abandon all sense of safety when I ride the bumpy tractor-pulled wagon and fling a half-eaten apple across the gravel road.

For people who are poor and hungry, however, the apple season is not always so sweet and bountiful. At a recent field trip with some of our temple members to Eckert's Country Farm in Belleville, Illinois, families learned why the act of sharing our harvest is a *mitzvot*. After we pay for our apples, our group gathers under a red and white striped tent to prepare yummy apple crisps for the Jewish Food Pantry.

As the adults and kids work together to peel the skins, measure cups of brown sugar, and chop the apples, we carry out the *mitzvot* of "*peah, leket* and *shich'chach*." According to Jewish tradition, we are supposed to leave a corner of the field to be gleaned by the widows, orphans, and the poor. When we assemble the crumb-topped apple treats in aluminum pans, we understand in a tangible way how this *mitzvot* to leave the gleanings actually feeds the hungry.

In fact, the Torah contains a number of *mitzvot* to allow the poor to benefit from the agricultural yield of landowners. For example, in Leviticus, it tells us, "When you reap the harvest of your land, you shall not reap all the way to the edges of your field or gather the gleanings of your harvest. You shall not pick your vineyard bare, or gather the fallen fruit of your vineyard; you shall leave them for the poor and the stranger."

Here are a few favorite apple recipes to share with family, friends, neighbors, and local food banks.

Applesauce

4 pounds very red baking apples, peeled and cored
1 lemon
1 handful of Red Hot candies (for color and taste)
1 c. apple juice, cider, or water
Honey or maple syrup to taste

Cut the apples and lemon in quarters. Place in a heavy pot with the Red Hots. Add the liquid. Cover the pot, bring to a boil, and simmer over low heat, stirring occasionally to turn the apples and make sure they don't stick. Add more liquid as needed. Cook about 20 minutes or until the apples are soft. Let cool.

Put the sauce through a food processor and adjust the flavor by adding honey or maple syrup to taste. Refrigerate until ready to serve.

Granny Char's Apple Crisp

Filling:
5 to 6 tart apples (like Granny Smith) peeled, cored, and cut into ¾ inch slices. (If you use sweet apples you can add 1 t. of lemon juice to cut down on sweetness.)
2 T. granulated sugar

2 T. lightly packed brown sugar
1 t. cinnamon
¼ t. nutmeg
2 T. unsalted butter, melted

Topping:
¾ c. plus 2 T. all-purpose flour
¼ c. plus 2 T. old-fashioned oatmeal
¼ c. plus 3 T. granulated sugar
¼ c. plus 3 T. lightly packed brown sugar
12 T. unsalted butter, cut into small pieces and slightly softened

Preheat oven to 375 degrees. In a large bowl, toss apple slices with both sugars and the spices. Let sit for 20 minutes or until the apples release some juice and the sugar is moist.

Meanwhile, combine flour, oatmeal, and both sugars for the topping in a bowl and mix well with your fingertips, crumbling any lumps. Add the butter and work the mixture gently until it resembles coarse crumbs. Cover and refrigerate until ready to use. Transfer the apples and their juices to a one-quart casserole. Pour the melted butter over the apples. Sprinkle the topping evenly over them. Bake for 30 to 40 minutes, until the topping is golden brown and the filling is bubbling. Serve warm. Serves 4 to 6.

Forbidden Fruit Sweetens Rosh Hashanah

With a year-round cycle of major and minor holidays, Jewish people have plenty of opportunities to count their blessings and be thankful. After all, we're lucky enough to celebrate at least one festive occasion in every season, including Rosh Hashanah in the fall, Hanukkah in the winter, Passover in the spring, and *Tu B'Av* (like a Jewish Valentine's Day) in the summer. Plus, with all the religious traditions and rituals in between, from

Sukkot to *Shavuot*, we always have a holy excuse to go off our diets. That's right, the symbolic Jewish calendar is filled with reasons to party and nosh on foods that are as mouthwatering as they are meaningful.

For example, the New Year kicks off with traditional favorites like apple noodle koogle, followed by creamy blintze soufflé when we break the fast. After that, we look forward to latkes when we light the menorah, prune hamantaschen when we shake the *gragger*, *charoset* when we join a seder, and brisket soaked in lots of onions and savory juices whenever we get the chance. Throughout the year, we also savor bowls of matzo ball soup, whether our family's recipe makes the Jewish dumplings light and fluffy or hard as a rock. The matzo ball has got to be the ultimate comfort food, not counting bagels and cream cheese, of course.

Rosh Hashanah sets the precedent for Jewish cuisine at its finest. With the first blast of the *shofar*, Rosh Hashanah announces a New Year and the birthday of our world, which means we get to have our honey cake and eat it, too. It's a *mitzvah*—a commandment and a wonderful Jewish tradition—to begin Rosh Hashanah with a special meal that tastes like a traditional five-course Shabbat dinner, only sweeter.

I realize this is a stretch, but ever since Adam and Eve ate from the forbidden tree of knowledge, the apple has never lost its appeal and remains a key ingredient. At Rosh Hashanah, which begins on the first day of the Hebrew month of *Tishrei*, children and adults dip apples in honey. The fresh apple represents renewal; the natural honey symbolizes a sweet and prosperous New Year. The Jews have a blessing for everything, including fruit, which is *Borei Pri HaEtz*, followed by the words "*Yehi Ratzon…shetehadesh allenyu shanah tovah umetukah*," which means "May it be Your will to renew for us a good and sweet year."

At Yom Kippur, the apple serves yet another purpose for those who observe the fast. Children can poke whole cloves into an apple—they can make a pattern if they wish—and bring the fruit with you to synagogue to ward off feelings of faintness. Whenever you feel a hunger pang, sniff the fragrant spice and see what happens.

Everything tastes sweeter at Rosh Hashanah—even the round challah when it's sprinkled with chewy raisins and dipped in honey. Unlike the rest of the year, the crown-like shape symbolizes the cycle of the year and God's kingship over the people of Israel. The cyclical shape also represents wholeness and our desire for a well-rounded and complete New Year.

At this time of year, I get into my Martha Stewart mode and dig out old and new apple recipes, from cakes and casseroles to salads and salsas. On a crisp, autumn day, one of my favorite family outings is apple picking at a local orchard. If the bees don't chase us away first, we load our baskets with juicy apples that we sample along the way. Back home, I arrange a variety in a bowl for a colorful kitchen table centerpiece. By the time we share the crop with family and neighbors, the fruit disappears in a hurry. But before that happens, I cook my own applesauce with a pinch of cinnamon.

Sari eats apples and honey year round, so we like to concoct something extra special at Rosh Hashanah. Together, we dip the tart apples in melted caramel and then roll them in pecans or candies that we crush ahead of time with a rolling pin. We like to use mini M&Ms, toffee pieces, and chocolate chips. I let the apples cool on a cookie sheet or pan that I line with waxed paper and grease with cooking spray.

On the second day of Rosh Hashanah, it's customary to try a fruit that we've never eaten before, such as a kiwano melon, prickly pear, or even a coconut. Of course, the pomegranate is a popular biblical fruit also eaten on this holiday. The deep pink fruit symbolizes fertility and prosperity because of its numerous seeds—613 inside each one, in fact, to correspond with the 613 *mitzvot* incumbent upon each Jew. By the way, the prayer over the pomegranate seeds is, "May our merits multiply like pomegranate seeds."

Apple recipes are easy to come by, but here are a couple of my Rosh Hashanah favorites, including a colossal cake that could fill the belly of the biblical whale that swallowed Jonah.

Apple Raisin Koogle

12 oz. bag of noodles
3 eggs beaten
4 T. sugar
¼ t. cinnamon (or more)
Pinch salt
1 ¼ c. grated apple (I like tart)
½ c. white raisins
4 T. melted butter

Boil and drain noodles. In bowl, combine eggs, sugar, cinnamon, and salt. Set aside. Add apples, raisins, and melted butter to cooked noodles. Mix all ingredients thoroughly. Place in large, well-greased casserole. Bake at 350 degrees for 45 minutes.

Pineapple Applesauce Cake

Step 1: In large bowl, mix following three ingredients for 15 minutes:
1 c. oil
3 c. sugar
3 eggs

Step 2: Sift dry ingredients in separate bowl:
2 T. baking soda
2 T. cinnamon
6 c. flour

Step 3: Pour liquid ingredients in separate bowl:
1 large can unsweetened applesauce
1 can crushed pineapple (2 ½ c. size can)
½ c. water
2 T. vanilla

Alternate dry ingredients in step two and liquid ingredients in step three into the mixture of step one. Pour into greased 24-cup gelatin ring mold. Let stand in pan for a few minutes. Bake at 350 degrees for 60-70 minutes.

Fasting Makes Jews Hungry For More

One of my favorite parts about being Jewish, aside from the rich traditions and ancient wisdom that are passed down to us, is our "it's-all-about-the-food" attitude. This expression is especially true on holidays, lifecycle events, and pretty much any given meal.

So on the one day of the year when Jews are asked to fast, Yom Kippur, I'm almost relieved to have a chance to cleanse my palette and my soul before I reach for another slice of honey cake. That doesn't mean that the 24-hour stretch of self-denial is easy for me. Not even close. Anything can tempt my taste buds, from when I watch Sari pour herself a bowl of granola to when I come across a stale stick of Big Red chewing gum at the bottom of my purse. When I hear Jack sneak into the pantry and tear into a plastic bag of something salty and crunchy, I start to shake and sweat. When that happens, I try to spend time outdoors and take Luci for a walk before the dried nuggets in her stainless steel bowl start to look appetizing.

Another good way to distract me from being hungry is to pray at temple. At least there I know the people around me can relate to my empty stomach and my need for spiritual fulfillment. Together, we reflect, contemplate, and pray individually and as a community. Our grumbling bellies remind us why we are there. We also see each other in a new light, especially many of the women who don't wear makeup, jewelry, or leather handbags. Yom Kippur, which is considered the most important day in the Jewish calendar, is a time for purity when we focus on our inner selves, not our outward appearance. (Good thing this repentance ritual is only once a year.)

Even though my children are too young to fulfill the commandment to fast because they are under the *bar* and *bat mitzvah* age of 13, they can still participate in Yom Kippur in their own way. That's when I ask Jack and Sari to give up something they like for the Day of Atonement. For my 12-year-old son, a single day without video games is enough to send him into shock. Plus, without the remote control and animated racecars, he has a lot more free time to think about any regrets he has over the past year and how he can make the situation better in the New Year ahead. For my 8-year-old daughter, a day without cookies is a wake-up call to focus on the times when she and her brother often fight and how she can resolve those conflicts better next time.

At this solemn time of remembrance and atonement, families with children can do many activities together. We can visit the cemetery where a loved one is buried and share memories of that person. We also can give *tzedakah* as part of healing the soul. Another way to get into the spirit is to make a Wall of Forgiveness that simulates the *Kotel*, or Western Wall. Here's how:

Take a large sheet of brown or white paper or even wrapping paper, and hang it somewhere special in your home. Then, make tiny slits in the paper. Use another small piece of paper to write your personal thoughts of something that you want to be forgiven for. Everyone in the family takes a turn, even the younger children, who can draw a picture instead of writing words. Next, tuck the folded piece of paper inside the slit to demonstrate the powerful act of forgiveness and what this holiday is all about.

The Wall of Forgiveness helps parents teach their children that we all make mistakes and that God gives us another chance to become better people. For me, the most powerful message is that God forgives us for sins against God, but the hurts against other people are not forgiven until we have made peace with them.

This is a hard lesson to swallow, unlike the golden brown cheese blintzes topped with a dollop of sour cream.

A Jewish Thanksgiving? That's No Jive Turkey

Is it just me, or does anyone else out there feel the stress of you-know-what around the corner? It seems to me that the winter holiday season, also known as Hanukkah Hysteria or December Dilemma, sneaks up on us earlier each year. No sooner do I unplug the jack-o'-lantern and polish off the Halloween Tootsie Rolls does our gentile society suck us into their world: Santas at every shopping mall, Jingle Bells on every radio station, and gigantic wreaths and red velvet ribbons tied around every light post in town. No wonder I find myself singing "Winter Wonderland" in the shower.

My point here is that even though I fully participate in all sorts of merriment, including decking my own halls with festive blue and white lights, I try not to get too carried away until at least after Thanksgiving. This favorite American celebration, which honors the feast shared by Native Americans and English settlers in the Massachusetts colony so long ago, deserves its full day of glory without any other holiday distractions.

So, on that note, let's talk turkey. Even though Thanksgiving is not a Jewish holiday, or even a religious one, it is the most American of holidays, and Jews love it because we get to eat all day and give thanks without having to go to temple. Actually, Thanksgiving might as well be a Jewish holiday because of the similar themes. In Deuteronomy we are told, "When you have eaten your fill, give thanks." Also, the Israelites suffered famine and hardships, just as the earliest pioneers did, only the Jews reaped their bounty in the Land of Milk and Honey long before the Pilgrims landed on Plymouth Rock.

Jewish people even have a prayer for Thanksgiving. The birkat ha-mazon, the blessing for providing food, is one of the most important prayers and one of the very few that the Bible commands us to say. In part, it says: "Blessed are You, Adonai our God, King of the Universe, who nourishes the entire world with His goodness, with favor, with kindness, and with mercy. He provides food for all flesh, for his kindness endures forever. And through His great goodness, we have never lacked and we will not lack food forever and ever, for the sake of His great Name…"

With the focus on delicious food, there are many ways to bring out the Jewish flavor of Thanksgiving. In fact, in addition to a kosher turkey, other Jewish cuisine easily adapts to the feast. My Aunt Syl, who is my mom's younger sister, used to make an old-fashioned challah stuffing that disappeared from the table as fast as a chicken with its head cut off.

Not until years later did I learn why this favorite dish tasted so uniquely rich. Even though the recipe is now barely readable on a torn, yellowish piece of paper from a 50-year-old Jewish cookbook, my aunt vividly recalls how the night before Thanksgiving she laid out challah slices on her dining room table. The next day, she toasted both sides of the bread directly on the oven rack and broke the crispy challah into pieces. Some of the main ingredients are the same as in modern recipes and include chicken broth, eggs, celery, onion, salt, pepper, and paprika. Plus, my aunt added a grated potato and instead of using healthy vegetable oil, she went for the cholesterol-laden good stuff—schmaltz and gribenis, chicken skin that is rendered in a sauce pan until it's crispy, then seasoned with salt and pepper and mixed with chopped onions.

Another Jewish cuisine that is perfect for Thanksgiving is *tzimmes*, a saucy combination of carrots and pineapple that introduces dried cranberries in place of the usual prunes.

Tradition is an essential ingredient in all Jewish holidays and the Thanksgiving meal is no exception. When it comes to making a turkey, no one has a better *schtik* than my hilarious father-in-law Norman, who massages and sings to "Tom the Turkey" before sliding the 22-pound bird into the oven. With his grandchildren as his audience, he really puts on a show. He belts out his best Yiddish opera voice and massages the outside and inside of the turkey with a secret mixture that includes olive oil, minced garlic, salt, garlic salt, and pepper. Then, he stuffs the turkey with carrots, onions, celery, and sometimes throws in an apple, orange, or other citrus fruit for a zesty flavor.

A Jewish twist makes any holiday more meaningful. In between bites of candied sweet potatoes, you can share stories about how different family members at your table found freedom in America, going back to the earliest generations. Also, it's a *mitzvah* to feed others; invite someone far from home to share

Thanksgiving with you. Other ways for Jews to show their thanks is to serve food at a community Thanksgiving dinner for the needy, deliver meals to shut-ins, or donate money to an organization that fights hunger.

Tu Bishvat Celebrates Symbolic Fruits And Nuts

Leave it to ancient and modern Jews to milk another holiday—*Tu Bishvat*—for all its glory. *Tu Bishvat*, also known as the New Year or birthday for trees, raises our awareness of the environment. On top of that, *Tu Bishvat* is also called Feast of Fruits, which celebrates the native and abundant delicacies of the land of Israel.

Sounds like a good excuse to satisfy my sweet tooth.

Tu Bishvat occurs in the middle of winter in the United States, but around the same time in Israel, the *shekediyah*, or almond tree, shows the first hint of spring with pink and white flowers. To commemorate the miracle of nature and another bountiful harvest, Jews everywhere wine and dine on special fruits and nuts as part of their *Tu Bishvat* seder.

In medieval times, kabbalists, Jewish mystics, considered special treats like almonds, dates, figs, wheat, barley, pomegranates, and avocado both succulent and spiritual. They believed that inside a fruit or nut is a seed that represents new life and potential growth. Likewise, that same divine presence is hidden inside all human beings. On *Tu Bishvat*, it became customary to enjoy foods like olives, honey, oranges, and kiwi as a symbolic way of releasing this divine energy or God's presence in the world. Carob is another traditional food eaten on *Tu Bishvat* since it traveled well from Israel to faraway lands.

Today, the *Tu Bishvat* seder is an appetizing way to introduce
your family to new tastes and traditions. In between eating fruits
and nuts, adult celebrants drink four cups of wine and say special
blessings. The first cup contains white wine, which symbolizes
the dormancy of winter. Gradually, red wine is added to each
subsequent glass to indicate the full bloom of spring. For a non-
alcoholic toast, try a mixture of apple juice, white grape juice,
cherry juice, pomegranate juice, or cranberry juice.

In addition to reading stories about nature, participants can
recite these *Tu Bishvat* blessings:

Before each cup of wine, say: *"Baruch Atah Adonai Eloheinu
Melech Ha'olam borei p'ree ha-gafen.* You bound in Blessings,
Adonai Our God. You create the fruit of the vine."

Before eating fruit, say: *"Barauh tah Adonai, Eloheinu Melech
Ha'olam, borei p'ree ha'eitz.* Holy One of Blessing. Your Presence
fills creation; creating the fruit of the vine."

When you see a tree in blossom for the first time in spring, say:
*"Baruch Atah Adonai, Eloheinu Melech Ha'olam, shelo hisar
meolamo davar, uvarah vo briyot tovot veilanot tovim, lehanot bahem
benai adam.*

Holy One of Blessing. Your Presence fills Creation; You left
nothing lacking in Your world, and created in it goodly creatures
and beautiful trees to delight people's hearts."

Also, to celebrate *Tu Bishvat,* try a new recipe with Israeli
specialty foods, including this scrumptious dessert or breakfast
treat that combines the look of a winter snowflake with the
sweet taste of spring.

Israeli Date Cake

In a large mixing bowl, pour:
½ c. boiling water over 1 pound chopped dates
Add:
2 c. chopped pecans or walnuts
1 c. sugar
2 T. butter
Beat slightly:
2 eggs
Add to other ingredients.
Mix together in another bowl:
3 ½ c. flour
2 t. baking soda
¼ c. carob powder or cocoa (optional)
Add to wet ingredients.
Add:
2 t. vanilla
Dash cinnamon

Bake in lightly greased 9 x 13 pan at 350 degrees for about one hour. Do not overcook. Allow to cool before serving. To make snowflake decoration on top, place a large doily over the cake. Dust with powdered sugar then very carefully remove the doily.

Tu Bishvat And The Super Bowl

I'm not a football fan, except when the Rams win the Super Bowl, but I get excited about any sporting or entertainment event that gives my family an excuse to eat in front of the television. Besides the Super Bowl, the only other show that justifies crumbs on my family room carpet is the season finale of

American Idol. Let's face it—the big game calls for some seriously playful finger food. Best of all, since the nation's biggest sporting spectacle falls on the same weekend as *Tu Bishvat,* why not extend the fruit eating ritual one more day and give everyone something truly unique and exciting to nibble on?

Here's an idea for an edible fruit tree that's as much fun to make as it is to munch. Plus, this colorful display of natural sweets is a conversation piece, which comes in handy for me since I have nothing to say about the Colts and Bears anyway.

Your kids will love to help make this project, while they choose their favorite fruits or even try new ones to decorate the tree. To get started, you need the following supplies:

- Cone-shaped foam
- Circle-shaped foam
- Glue
- Lots of frilly toothpicks
- Green leaf lettuce, clean and dry
- Assorted fruit, cleaned and cut into bite-sized pieces
- Large serving platter
- Chocolate fondue (optional)

To make the structure of the tree, start with two pieces of foam—one in the shape of a cone and another circular shape for the base. You can buy foam pieces, which are available in different sizes, at any craft store. Put a few dots of white glue or craft glue on the bottom of the cone piece and press firmly to the center of the circle. Allow to dry for several hours or overnight.

When the foam pieces are securely attached, you're ready to cover the entire structure with green leaf lettuce. First, use frilly toothpicks to carefully poke the leaves into the entire foam structure, including the base, until the tree is covered in vibrant green. Next, use a toothpick to attach each individual bite-size fruit, such as strawberries, blueberries, melons, apricots, oranges, bananas, grapes, cherries, kiwi, apples, dates, and whatever you like. In addition to fresh fruit, you also can use dried and canned fruit.

Place your favorite chocolate fondue next to the fruit tree for an extra sweet treat.

According to kabbalistic mystics, fruit is a metaphor for God, which makes the *Tu Bishvat* seder highly symbolic. For example, celebrants eat three groups of up to 10 kinds of fruits and nuts. The first group consists of fruits and nuts with a hard outside shell that can't be eaten, such as nuts with an outer shell, pomegranates, and coconuts. The second group has a soft outside but an inedible pit, such as olives, dates, cherries, apricots, plums, and peaches. The third category is wholly edible, such as grapes, figs, apples, pears, raspberries, blueberries, and carobs.

Each of these groupings represents an increasingly closer relation to God, but on Super Bowl Sunday, it's the guys in the helmets who need our prayers.

Shavuot **Kicks Off Summer**

Summer doesn't mean that the Jewish holidays are on vacation. Think again. One of the most significant events in Jewish history—the giving of the Torah at Sinai—occurs seven weeks after Passover and celebrates the cutting of the harvest of wheat and first fruits in Israel. The joyous holiday known as *Shavuot*, which means "weeks" in Hebrew, doesn't get the widespread recognition of Hanukkah or share any distinctive symbols, such as matzo and a *sukkah*, like the other two pilgrimage holidays of Passover and *Sukkot*. However, without *Shavuot*, our journey to the Promised Land is incomplete, like the ultimate cliffhanger. Without *Shavuot*, there would be no dramatic liberation at Passover. The festival of *Shavuot* not only gives us the conclusion to the story of the exodus from Egypt, but also much to be thankful for.

On the day that God revealed the Ten Commandments to Moses, the dry, desert mountain burst into a green pasture and bloomed with flowers, which is why we decorate our synagogue and home with greenery and flowers. Also, *Shavuot* commemorates when the Jewish people were given the oral and written laws, including *kashrut*, or kosher dietary laws that authorize them to eat dairy foods. Before the revelation of the Ten Commandments, Jews didn't keep kosher. Today we celebrate this historical event by enjoying an array of dietary delights, as well as reading the Ten Commandments. The Bible says, "And God gave us this land, a land flowing with milk and honey."

To acknowledge the ancient agricultural aspect of *Shavuot*, which is also called *Hag Hakatzir*, Festival of the (wheat) Harvest, and *Yom HaBikurim*, Day of the First Fruits, families are encouraged to go green. Prior to the holiday, you can turn your home into a greenhouse and decorate with ornamental fruit trees, branches, wildflowers, and grasses. To make pretty centerpieces, arrange wicker baskets with fresh fruit and fill vases with colorful cut flowers from your garden. Spice up the rooms with bowls of potpourri and, as in old European tradition, hang roses in windows facing the street. No wonder children love this holiday, especially in Israel where the youngsters wear floral wreaths around their heads. To get into the spirit, Sari and I like to make necklaces out of sweet smelling honeysuckle vines and tuck daisies behind our ears.

As with any Jewish holiday, food is symbolic. The custom on *Shavuot* is to eat dairy foods like blintzes, cheesecake, koogels, cream cheese, boukeas (Sephardic-filled leaf dough pastry), and cheese-filled kreplach. Other dairy delicacies include ice cream sundaes, cheese enchiladas, and vegetarian lasagna.

A real treat to make on *Shavuot* is a modern version of a seven-layer cake that goes back to a custom among the Sephardim, Jews of Spanish or Portuguese origin. The seven-layer cake is called *Siete Cielos*, or Seven Heavens, which symbolizes the seven celestial spheres that God traveled in order to present the Torah to Moses on Mount Sinai.

A three-tiered Mount Sinai cake works just as well and is a lot easier to make. Start with a loaf-shaped pound cake. You can buy one already made or bake one from scratch. Cut the cake into three pieces: small, medium, and large. Place the big layer on the bottom, and make three tiers like blocks in a tower. Cover the cake with whipped cream and garnish with strawberries and a few mint springs for greenery. Finally, decorate the top with a Jewish symbol, such as a Star of David or paper cut in the shape of the tablets of the Ten Commandments.

Shavuot is a unique Jewish holiday, and so are the foods that go along with it. In honor of the land of "milk and honey," dairy delicacies with a touch of sweetness are on the menu. Try this favorite koogel recipe from my friend Jamie.

Jamie's Cheesy Apricot Koogle

1 8 oz. package of fine noodles
1 c. apricot nectar
½ c. sugar
3 eggs
3 oz. cream cheese (softened)
½ c. milk
¾ stick of butter (softened)

For the topping:

½ c. brown sugar

½ stick melted butter

1 c. cornflake crumbs

Boil noodles – don't over cook. Combine all ingredients in a
bowl, then pour into a greased 9 x 13 glass dish. Mix together the
topping and spread on top. Bake at 325 degrees for 1 hour.

Chocolate Makes Every Day Sweeter

When it comes to Valentine's Day, if I had to choose, I'd rather
my husband give me chocolate than long-stemmed red roses,
unless the flowers are the edible kind. Diamonds may be a girl's
best friend, but chocolate is her secret lover.

A week before Valentine's Day, I bought a box of Russell Stover
at the grocery store to give as a gift to my daughter, who also loves
chocolate (it's hereditary). I knew as I went through the checkout
lane that it was a bad idea. Then again I stock up on Halloween
candy right after Labor Day knowing full well that the mini
Snickers won't last in the freezer until the end of October.

When I got home, I put away the apples and broccoli and I
stashed the chocolates in a drawer in the china cabinet. (That's
a trick I got from my mom.) I figure out of sight out of mind,
right? But as the pot of water boiled for spaghetti, I couldn't
control my cravings any longer. I snuck into the dining room and
ripped open the plastic wrap. My mouth watered as I admired the
coconut clusters. It wasn't long before little brown papers were
scattered on the carpet and the chocolate-covered almonds and
cherry nougats were gone. When my family later asked me why I
wasn't hungry for dinner, I fessed up. I'm on a diet.

Eating chocolate makes me happy, and science proves it. Cocoa phenols, or flavonoids, in chocolate are shown to lower blood pressure and balance certain hormones in the body. Moreover, dark chocolate contains a large number of antioxidants (nearly eight times the amount found in strawberries), which is why chocolate-covered strawberries are the answer to better cardiovascular health. Also, a study conducted by the Hershey Center for Health and Nutrition indicates that cocoa powder in dark chocolate has even more antioxidants than pomegranate. Experts also believe that chocolate helps fight cancer, which is why I eat only chocolate macaroons on Passover.

In other words, it makes perfect sense that Valentine's Day is in February, which is also Heart Health Month.

For true chocolate connoisseurs, the history of chocolate and how it's made is fascinating. Of course, the Jews had a hand in the discovery of this wonderful food. In fact, along with Christopher Columbus (who might have been Jewish), the Jews brought the fabrication of chocolate to France in the 17th century, and they played a vital role in the early production and distribution of chocolate in Europe. No one knows more about the rich relationship between Jewish people and chocolate than Rabbi Deborah Prinz and her husband Rabbi Mark Hurvitz, who travel the world studying chocolate (the best job) and write a blog called "Jews on the Chocolate Trail."

Their blog lists lots of tasty tidbits:

- Woody Guthrie wrote a song about Hanukkah *gelt*.
- North American Jewish colonial traders were involved in the chocolate trade.
- The popular Israeli chocolate company, Max Brenner, is owned by the Israeli food conglomerate Elite Strauss.
- Jewish values such as *oshek* (honest and fair labor practices)

and *bal taschit* (saving that which has potential for future use) should be considered when selecting chocolate.

• We could (and should) add chocolate into more Jewish rituals and celebrations, such as a chocolate seder and chocolate-covered matzo.

Now I'll drink to that, as long as its red wine. In fact, the anti-aging ingredient resveratrol found in red wine thins blood and reduces the incidence of heart attack and stroke. It gets even better. In addition to enjoying the health benefits of chocolate and red wine for Valentine's Day, it turns out that flowers, especially the scent of roses, improve mood, anxiety, skin aliments, and sleep. And while I'm on the subject of ecstasy, sex is scientifically proven to have 10 times the anxiety/muscle spasm-reducing effect of Valium.

But don't tell my husband.

Chapter 5
The December Dilemma -
Hanukkah or Chanukah?

Hanukkah Means Freedom Of Expression

If there's one thing Jews can agree on, it's that Hanukkah is
not a Jewish Christmas. (Now getting us to agree on how to
spell Hanukkah is another story.) Sure, both holidays occur in
December and fulfill lots of children's wishes, but the similarities
between Hanukkah and Christmas stop there.

Actually, Hanukkah ranks as a minor festival compared to the
other High Holidays. Still, the Festival of Lights is a favorite
holiday on the Jewish calendar. I mean, come on, presents for
eight days straight? Who wouldn't want to be a Jew this time of
year? Hanukkah is not the kind of holiday that is worshipped
in a special synagogue service, however. Hanukkah is mostly
celebrated at home, where we light the menorah, say special
blessings, eat latkes, spin the dreidel, and sing songs. For some
families, another tradition is to dedicate their time and effort to
a social action project, such as delivering toys or serving meals to

the needy, which is what *tikkun olam* is all about.

The origin of Hanukkah, which means "dedication," dates back more than 2,000 years when the Greek king Antiochus tried to force the Jews to pray his way, to the gods of Greece. But the Jews refused because they believed in their own God of Israel. To save the Jewish people's religious freedom, a small band of soldiers, called the Maccabees, fought against Antiochus and his mighty Greek army. The Maccabees were brave heroes, ordinary people armed with little more than their faith in God. Their courageous victory marked the first miracle of Hanukkah and taught us a very powerful lesson that still applies today— Jews and non-Jews alike must defend their freedom of religious expression.

The second miracle happened after the Maccabees and the people of Jerusalem started to clean up the Temple that the Greek army had destroyed. The Maccabees removed all traces of idol worship and spent eight days rededicating the Jewish holy place. Although the original Hebrew texts related to Hanukkah have been lost, legend has it that the Maccabees discovered a small flask of oil to light the seven-branched gold candelabrum. The lamp oil was supposed to last for only one day. When the oil in the menorah burned for eight days, it was considered another miracle and is the other reason why we celebrate the Festival of Lights for eight days.

No wonder light is the symbol of our festival celebration. Personally, I take the concept of Festival of Lights even further when I decorate the inside and outside of my home with blue and white lights, which are the colors of the Israeli flag. Mostly, I cherish my collection of menorahs, called *chanukiyahs*, including a marble one in the shape of a spiraling staircase that my mom bought me in Israel and another wax-covered, whale-shaped candleholder that Jack and Great Grandma Ruth sculpted themselves out of clay. I realize that some Jewish people may say "Feh!" to my holiday lights tradition that I started when Sari was born on Christmas Eve almost eight years ago, but then again, Jews argue about the spelling of the braided loaf of white bread. Is it challah, challeh, or halla anyway?

The reason why I choose to hang lights, in addition to displaying an array of silver and gold dreidels, is to make Sari's birthday special and fulfill my own childhood fantasies during the winter season. In fact, ever since Sari was a toddler, I told her that the twinkling lights on all the houses and trees were birthday candles and special wishes just for her. Even as a child, she never bought the idea. But the little kid in me likes all the lights, especially in the dark, when the glistening white snow covers the ground and branches. The lights put me in the holiday spirit, as I grip the wobbly ladder that Scott hesitantly climbs so that he can reach the gutter of our two-story house. When another big blue bulb breaks in his bare hand, I try to ignore his curse words and quickly fetch another replacement before he changes his mind about the whole thing.

Even though my blue and white holiday lights have nothing to do with being Jewish, the festive decorations represent my freedom of expression. Along with the flickering candles on the menorah, the lights remind me of the miracles long ago and who I am today. A proud Jew.

Menorah Lights The Way For Future Generations

The Jewish people are a "light unto the nations" and our mission to keep the miracle alive is never brighter than at Hanukkah when the flickering candles on the menorah symbolize hope and joy. Each time we light a candle, we are reminded of the possibility of miracles in our lives. We remember that in a time of darkness our ancestors had the courage to struggle for freedom—freedom to be themselves, freedom to worship in their own way.

Growing up, I thought that lighting the menorah was the symbol to eat dinner and get a present. It's actually a *mitzvah* to light the menorah and to display the nine-branch candelabrum in a window for everyone to see and be uplifted by the glow. This *mitzvah* is known in Hebrew as *pirsum ha'nes*, or "publicizing the miracle." We celebrate the miracle of the oil, the miracle of the victory of the weak over the strong, and the miracle of the few against the mighty. Finally, we affirm the miracle of the survival of the Jewish nation against the odds, which is as real today as it was more than 2,000 years ago.

The ritual of lighting the candles is significant as well. We place candles in the menorah from right to left, and we light them from left to right. In other words, we place them in English, and we kindle them in Hebrew. Each night a new candle is added toward the left.

The newest candle is lit first so every candle gets a chance to be first. The tallest candle, the *shamash*, is used to light the other candles. The *shamash* occupies the highest position not because of its importance but because it serves others. *Shamash* means "servant" or "helper." It's customary to light the candles right after sundown. On Shabbat the candles are lit before the Sabbath begins. On Saturday night, the Hanukkah candles are lit after *Havdalah*.

Each night, the following two blessings are recited as the candles are lit: "Blessed are You, Adonai our God, ruler of the universe, who makes us holy with *mitzvot*, and who commands us to kindle the lights of Hanukkah."

And, "Blessed are You, Adonai, our God, ruler of the universe, who performed wondrous deeds for our ancestors in days of old, at this season."

On the first night of Hanukkah only, the following prayer is added: "Blessed are You, Adonai our God, ruler of the universe, for giving us life, for sustaining us, and for enabling us to celebrate this joyous season."

When I was a child, my family used to light a simple, silver menorah and it was exciting for my brother and me to take turns holding the candle. Today, many families have a menorah for each child, making their own Hanukkah traditions. I enjoy my collection of menorahs because each one has special meaning. I love to watch the colorful light bulbs blink on my tall turquoise menorah that used to decorate my childhood home.

Once a year, the special marble menorah from Israel is removed from my china cabinet and takes center stage in the family room. Last year I splurged on an expensive contemporary menorah, hand-sculpted in gold, copper, and marble, but the whale-shaped clay menorah that my son

Sari's birthday potato menorah, December 2010.

made in preschool with his Great Grandma Ruth is priceless. The tail is chipped and colorful wax covers the whale's long body, but we cherish this work of art.

Also unique and non-traditional is Sari's birthday candle menorah that she made out of a giant potato. That's right, my daughter spray-painted silver an Idaho spud in honor of her

10th birthday, which is on the fourth night of Hanukkah this year. She poked plastic birthday candleholders in a straight line in the middle of the potato, stacking three holders in the far-left side for the *shamash* candle. By the way, many of our grandparents used a potato for a menorah because that's all they could afford.

During the eight days of Hanukkah, these lights are sacred. We are supposed to behold their beauty and share the light with others. It's also customary to not occupy ourselves with work while the flames are burning and women in particular should abstain from household duties at this time in thanks to the active role of women in the Hanukkah story. So why am I doing the dishes?

Surviving The Holidays Requires Twists On Traditions

I've gotten smarter over the years, especially when it comes to preparing for Hanukkah. It's a miracle all right that I get everything done, from buying presents and baking cookies to planning parties and decorating my home. Hanukkah was never meant to emphasize such extravagant gift giving, but I can't help myself. Even though the true meaning of Hanukkah is seen in the light of the menorah, which reminds us to never take for granted our religious freedom, I overindulge anyway.

Fortunately, I've figured out a way to survive this hectic time of year. Go on a cruise. Nah, just kidding. All it takes is a little creativity and preparation.

For one thing, I no longer wait until the last minute to shop for presents. Depending on when the Festival of Lights falls on the calendar, I begin my buying spree around the time my jack-o'-lanterns grow fuzz on their shriveled grins. Usually the first items on my gift list are practical ones, such as cozy turtlenecks, furry socks, warm pajamas, brand new thermal underwear, and coordinating sets of hats, gloves, and scarves in preparation for the first sleigh ride of the season. I ignore the fact that Jack and Sari rarely wear appropriate winter clothing, especially anything decorated in stripes and polka dots. They'd rather freeze than look uncool.

Another trick I've learned is to wrap the presents as soon as I buy them and while I still have energy left to curl ribbon. I set up a gift-wrapping station in my closet and organize all my supplies, including plenty of wrapping paper with dreidels and stars, colorful tissues, gift bags, stickers, scissors, tape, nametags, and bows of all sizes. For a special touch, I try to decorate the top of each present with *gelt*, but sometimes I can't resist my sweet tooth and savor the chocolate coins for myself.

After I wrap each trinket, I scribble a secret code, such as a word written backwards, on the bottom of the present. That way I don't forget what's hidden inside. For example, I write "emag oediv" for video game and "sffumrae" for earmuffs. Some letters are easier to decode than others, such as "dopi" for iPod. Usually my kids don't notice the clues because they're too distracted trying to guess the contents by shaking their presents violently. Sari, who is particularly observant, spots a word and tries to figure it out. I warn her that she's only spoiling her surprise. I need to come up with a better plan for next year, by the way, before my kids favor dyslexia.

I admit that my efficiency is sometimes a fault, and I get caught up in the excitement of the holiday. Instead of hiding the presents in a dark closet, this year I decided to display the beautifully wrapped packages around the fireplace before Hanukkah officially started. Big mistake. Everyday after school my kids recounted the presents in their piles and compared who got more. Not surprisingly, they nudged me to let them open one. When I noticed a torn piece of wrapping paper that covered one of Sari's gifts, she blamed our dog Luci. I don't know how people who celebrate Christmas leave all those presents under the tree for so long without any riots breaking out.

Another way that I try to make the holidays simpler is to spend less time in the kitchen and more quality time with family and friends. Although I like to cook, I gave up making latkes from scratch this year. In the past, I would grate potatoes until my knuckles bled and peel so many onions that I couldn't stop crying. Sure, the mouthwatering aroma of crisp potato pancakes sizzling in extra virgin olive oil is desirable for a day, but when the heavy, greasy smell permeates my hair, skin, clothes, and entire house for more than a week it's enough already. I understand that oil is most significant at Hanukkah. It symbolizes the miracle that the little cruse of oil in the temple burned brightly for eight days. Still, the fried foods, including *sufganiyot*, or jelly doughnuts, taunt my cholesterol.

So to make life a little simpler at Hanukkah time, I use frozen hash browns and add onions, eggs, and matzo meal. Better still, I buy frozen potato pancakes already made from the kosher butcher. I bake the golden brown latkes on a cookie sheet and save myself from washing so many fry pans. When topped with gobs of sour cream and applesauce nobody knows the difference.

Best of all, with these modern traditions, I have more time to spin the dreidel.

Get The Spin On The Dreidel Game

My dreidel collection seems to grow every year. The last time I counted, I had 67 tops in all sizes and colors. During the eight days of Hanukkah, I keep these inexpensive little toys in a decorative bowl on my coffee table right next to the stack of *Everyday With Rachael Ray* magazines.

The dreidel game is a wonderful family activity that never gets old. Then again, neither does chocolate gelt. I feel like a kid again when I flick my wrist in just the right way to make the wooden dreidel spin like a mini cyclone. I'm always up for a challenge when my kids want to see who can twirl their dreidel the longest or knock one off the table. So, dig into your piggy banks and purses and gather everyone's pennies. You also can use candy, raisins, nuts, tokens, or even count by points. It's time for some serious dreidel playing.

In case you need a refresher course on how to play the classic Hanukkah game, which was originally a popular Yiddish gambling activity, keep in mind these few simple rules. All players start with the same amount of coins or tokens, say 10. Everyone puts one token in the pot in the center. Each person, maybe youngest to oldest, takes turns spinning the dreidel. Whatever Hebrew letter lands facing up is what the player does.

For example: *Nun* means collect nothing; *Gimel* means take all the tokens in the pot; *Hay* means take half of the tokens; and *Shin* means the player puts one token in the kitty. Whoever ends up with all the loot or the most tokens is the winner. By the way, the Hebrew letters *Nun, Gimel, Hey,* and *Shin* supposedly stand for *"Nes Gadol Hayah Sham"* or "A Great Miracle Happened There."

In other words, the dreidel game is a great opportunity to learn about Jewish history. The word dreidel derives from the German *driehen* and means to spin. It originated more than 2,000 years ago as a way for Jews to hide their studying at a time when reading from the Torah was prohibited. In fact, Hanukkah celebrates the victory of the Jewish Maccabees over the Syrians, who banned all Jewish practices. If someone tried to read Jewish text or perform a Jewish ritual, such as a *bris*, they were sent to jail or killed. During this time of suppression, the clever Jewish people pretended to gamble when they were actually intellectualizing about their religion. So in modern times, families not only have fun together but they are expressing their religious freedom every time they spin the top.

For adults who want to kick the game up a notch, try using dimes and quarters and combining the activity with poker. Even though gambling is technically forbidden by the Jewish religion, the winner can donate his stash to charity, right?

Sharing The Bounty Brightens The Holiday

I knew Hanukkah was finally over when Jack flipped through the "Farmer's Almanac" that I gave him on day eight and searched for crisp dollar bills in between the pages of astronomical data. When Sari opened a box with a purple hoodie inside, I could tell by the disappointed look on her face that she rather would have a Limited Too gift card and pick out her own wardrobe. Even though I got a "Thanks mom" I didn't feel the love. Where's the true appreciation? I was disappointed by their selfish attitudes. Next year they're getting an orange in their tennis shoe like their Christian friends do on St. Nick's Day.

Growing up, I was thrilled to receive a brand new pair of knee-highs for Hanukkah. In fact, on the third candle I would get the left sock and on the fourth candle I would get the right one. I didn't know any different. When I became a mom, I somehow allowed Hanukkah to get out of hand over the years. It's my own fault. I buy so many presents that I forget where I hide all the wrapped packages. Just the other day I actually found under the couch a 2003 puppy calendar topped with a dusty silver bow.

Just like Christmas, Hanukkah can bring too much of a good thing. I mean how many furry Webkinz does a second grader really need? By giving our kids everything they want, parents are raising a spoiled generation that's always hungry for more. During the holiday season, adults overindulge as well. When I entertain, for example, I bake enough Swedish meatballs to feed an entire synagogue at the High Holidays. The latkes are devoured, but the cinnamon applesauce lasts way past the expiration date. If I didn't share my leftovers, I would be defrosting brisket until *Tu Bishvat* in late January.

So this year I vowed to do something different with my excess food and toys. The December gift-giving season provides endless opportunities to "light up" the world, otherwise known as *tikkun olam*, by sharing my abundance with others less fortunate.

Community soup kitchens are happy to receive cookies, casseroles, and whatever delicious leftover goodies I have that would otherwise end up in the freezer, garbage disposal, or my waistline. After New Year's, I've had my fill of Ritz crackers and cheddar cheese cubes, which are great snacks to share as well. Likewise, colorful holiday decorations and beautifully cut flowers still in bloom help brighten a nursing home or senior living facility. My kids usually get new coats and snow pants for Hanukkah, so the clothes they outgrow are donated to various nonprofit charities.

Also in need are new toys and books at local hospitals and children's homes. I have a closet full of board games that my kids rarely play with, so this time of year is a good excuse to clean house. I also encourage my kids to share some of their Hanukkah *gelt* (the green kind) and buy a little something for another boy or girl who has way less.

Make *Mitzvahs* The Centerpiece

Hanukkah is a time for *mitzvah*, but it is also, increasingly, a time for unreasonable gift lists from my kids. My grade-school daughter wants a $200 smartphone and my son wants a pair of Dr. Dre headphones that cost more than a month's car insurance premiums.

Parents are to blame for their children's spoiled behavior, and I'm certainly no exception. We stick our youngsters in front of the computer way too young, while they're still in diapers, and we practically give them a username and password by the time they get a social security card. No wonder today's youth have a constant need for stimulation and immediate gratification. When a recent Walmart television commercial advertises how Nintendo DS promotes family bonding, the situation is obviously out of control.

Jewish parents face a challenge every holiday season to resist the urge to give in to our children's unreasonable demands for things they don't really need. Is it necessary for my kids to have the latest and greatest electronic devices? Of course not. Do they need to hoard gift cards the same way my mother used to collect those lick-and-stick Eagle stamp books that she traded in for $2.50 at Famous-Barr? I don't think so.

It's our job as parents to teach our children from an early age about the real meaning of Hanukkah, which is to rededicate ourselves to others in need. While enjoying all the festivities of menorah lighting, latke eating, and present exchanges, it's also important to at least include the idea of giving and not just receiving. The best way to involve your family in a holiday *mitzvah* is to check out any local synagogue or social service

organization to find out how you can help make the holidays
brighter for someone who is going through tough times.

Jewish elves are in demand everywhere, especially in December,
whether you contribute to an adopt-a-family program at your
temple or children's school, sing holiday songs to residents at a
senior living center, serve dinner at your local Ronald McDonald
House, donate toys and warm clothes to the Salvation Army, wrap
gifts at a children's shelter, deliver meals to homebound elderly,
or use your unique skills to entertain or play an instrument with
patients at a children's hospital. So even if your child doesn't
get an iTouch for Hanukkah, the holiday is still filled with joy,
especially when we share our blessings with others.

Happy Hanukkah To All, And To All A Good Night

I dedicate this little poem to my daughter Sari, whose birthday
falls on December 24, and to all the other *boychiks* and *meydles*
who get ripped off every year because their December birthdays
are caught in the middle of the Hanukkah hoopla.

Twas the night before Christmas
When all through the hospital
Not a creature was stirring
Couldn't find a darn Popsicle.

My IV was hung
By my bedside with care,
In hopes that my doctor
Soon would be there.

Pregnant patients were nestled
All snug in their beds,
While visions of epidurals
Danced in their heads.

And grandma with her kerchief
And I in my gown,
Cursed every contraction
Like no one in town.

When outside the hallway
There arouse such a clatter,
"A Christmas babe is coming!"
Could I feel any fatter?

"My daughter is Jewish!"
I exclaimed as she fed.
So no red Santa hats
Atop her tiny bald head.

And so it began
That 24th day in December
Christmas is now a holiday
I'll always remember.

Chapter 6
The Life Of The Jewish Mother

All Moms Are Working Moms

I think mothers should be honored every day of the year, not just on Mother's Day. All moms are working moms. In fact, we define multi-tasking—just look at a typical day planner crammed with school functions, room mother meetings, activities, sports, doctor's appointments, birthday parties, grocery lists, babysitter phone numbers, and plenty of scratch-outs that signify that anything can change at any given moment. We don't get paid, but the experience makes us rich. We never retire, but the vacation time makes it all worthwhile.

I'm lucky. No, better than that, I'm blessed because I benefit from the companionship of my mom everyday, either on the phone or in person. She always listens to my parenting gripes and offers advice, whether I ask for it or not. One of her favorite lines—"You wanted to have kids…no one ever said it would be easy"— might sound unsympathetic, but it's so true. In fact, the

Hebrew phrase *"tzar gidul banim"* refers to the inevitable pain of raising children. The pain goes both ways. Parents suffer, children suffer, and, hopefully, the hardships we suffer together make us stronger.

One thing I discovered so far as a mom is to find humor whenever possible. The other thing I learned is that if I don't make lists of things to do, I forget to do them. So for the fun of it, here's my *not* to-do list. I will not:

1. Pluck pinfeathers from a kosher chicken, even if the soup tastes better.
2. Make my children clean all the food on their plates, unless they're loading them into the dishwasher.
3. Eat another frozen latke at a public menorah lighting ceremony.
4. Go through the day without doing one *mitzvah*, even if it means taking Luci for a walk when no one else wants to.
5. Make Christmas seem like more fun than Hanukkah.
6. Serve a corned beef sandwich on white bread with mayonnaise.
7. Wear a red and green holiday sweater that has a reindeer on it.
8. Shelter my children from the Holocaust when they are ready to learn about it.
9. Throw away my collection of handkerchief challah covers, clay menorahs, and bottle cap candlestick holders that my kids made in preschool.
10. Say no to my mom when she invites us to her house for brunch.
11. Stay mad at my kids for too long, at least until the next battle erupts.
12. Remain dry-eyed when I read a Mother's Day card made with colored markers and construction paper.

Happy Mother's Day!

I dedicate this column to all moms, especially mine because without her I wouldn't be here. If not for my mom, I wouldn't be born. Otherwise, my soul might have ended up in the physical body of a dolphin or an eagle or a peasant farmer in Mexico. But I wouldn't be me.

So, thanks mom. Thanks for everything you've done to me—I mean for me—over the years. Your unconditional love has helped shape the person who I am today. In fact, when Sari wants to know where I get my "*matzo tuchas*," I give you all the credit. Likewise, when my daughter giggles at her dimples in the mirror, I remind her to watch her Grandma Char smile.

Mom, you've taught me so much about life and how kind words and homemade chocolate chip cookies go a long way. You never forget to send a birthday card or wrap a present. From you I learned the importance of gratitude and a thank you note. Mom, you're a sweet, caring person. You enjoy being with others but don't mind being alone either. You always make time to share a cup of tea. You are forever cutting out coupons and articles for me.

You're not afraid to try new recipes, and you hooked me on the 24-hour Food Network. Plus, your mock chopped liver has become your signature dish. Even though you never can remember where you left your sunglasses, your mind is sharp, and you balance your checkbook and pay your bills without a calculator.

You're also not afraid to speak your mind and give your opinion. Plus, you continue to show me everyday that aging is all about attitude. You've been going to the Fox Theatre since you were a kid, and you still love musicals and plays. You're also a fan of Cardinals baseball and introduced Jack to cotton candy at his first Cardinals game at Busch Stadium when he was only three years old.

When it comes to the latest fashions, you're never too old to go shopping even though you would rather call capri pants pedal pushers, and for the longest time you referred to Dillard's as Stix. Not only that, I get more compliments on your hand-me-down tote bags.

Another valuable lesson that I learned from you is to always put the needs of my children first. For example, just like you, I hide the black liquorice nibs in the drawer of my dining room buffet table so that no one spoils their appetites. Even when I hear my kids open a candy wrapper from my disappearing secret stash, I keep the Hershey's kisses in the same place anyway. That's love.

Especially when it comes to your children and grandchildren, you celebrate every accomplishment, big and small. You still get excited every time Jack makes a base hit or Sari gets a perfect score on her spelling test or when a story of mine is published.

The older I get, the more I appreciate your wisdom and the end pieces of *kamish* bread. So thanks mom for everything, especially

My mom and I celebrate my 40th birthday, August 2004.

for giving me the *mishegas* of motherhood. Happy Mother's Day!

Thank Your Mother On Your Birthday

Every year, when my friend Rochelle celebrates her birthday she gives her mother a gift. Why? Well, why not?

Motherhood is usually a thankless job, so a little token of appreciation makes perfect sense, even if a mom has to wait until her child is a grownup to receive a present. When Rochelle blows out her birthday candles, she's not thinking about herself. She's thinking about her mother who endured labor without an epidural, which doesn't come close to the pain she suffered raising a teenage daughter.

This birthday gift-back is a mother-daughter tradition that began after Rochelle's first son Jeremy was born 14 years ago. It's a special way for Rochelle to say thanks to her mom for allowing her to experience the wonders of motherhood, including swollen feet during pregnancy, sleepless nights with a newborn, and prematurely gray hair over math homework. Mostly, it's a special way to say, "Mom, I love you."

Indeed, mothers and daughters have a special bond. Even though my daughter Sari is only 10, I already feel like we're intuitively connected. Often I know what she's thinking before she says a word. When she stares blankly at her closet full of clothes and can't find a thing to wear, I understand. When she blames the dryer for shrinking her jeans instead of the hot fudge sundae she ate the night before, I feel her pain. When it takes her half an hour to pick out liquid body soap because she has to smell each one, I wait patiently. And when her daddy says he likes her outfit but he really doesn't mean it, she sees right through her old man just like I can.

Indeed having a daughter is a gift, and I feel blessed that Sari and I already wear the same size shoes. Remember the saying, "A daughter is your daughter for life. A son is your son until he finds a wife…" (And she's never good enough for him anyway.)

Back To School: The Other High Holiday

For many parents, the highest of High Holidays occurs around the end of August when their kids go back to school. For me, this time of year truly kicks off my Days of Awe when I practice the three R's: reflect, repent, and revise.

First, I reflect on the highlights of the summer, including weekends at the lake with grandma and grandpa and riding in the giant tube. Second, I ask forgiveness for not exercising enough, unless floating on a raft counts. Third, I set personal goals for the new school year ahead, such as building my own website.

Let's face it. No matter how exciting our summer vacations, most moms are ready for a break from their kids by now. I can't possibly plan another fun thing that doesn't involve a trip to the ATM first. And the timing for school to start is perfect because with every passing day, I think Jack forgets how to spell another word. Besides, my tube of sunscreen is almost empty, so why not get into the mode of homework, lunch bags, and carpool lines?

This year, however, evokes more anxiety for me than usual because my oldest child starts middle school. My biggest concern, other than how to train a night owl to wake up at the crack of dawn, is how can one kid remember so many numbers in a single day? Somehow Jack has already memorized the combination for his locker, which I think requires the skill of Houdini to crack open. To recall the locker combination, Jack associates the numbers with baseball players and then gives the locker a quick punch. Moreover, he has to keep straight another code for gym class, a p.i.n. if he wants to eat lunch, and still more numbers if he wants to make his way home on the bus. I never would survive middle school because I barely can remember my garage keypad numbers. Even when I just have to press a button, I still forget to turn off my windshield wipers once I'm inside the garage.

Just as Jack enters a new stage in school, I begin a new phase of motherhood. This momentous event didn't really hit me until I shopped for items on his school supply list that didn't include crayons but a scientific calculator instead. I spent hours in the crowded aisles trying to figure out the colors and widths on the pocket binders and I'm still not convinced I got it right. Plus, I didn't realize until I got home that I bought college-lined instead of wide-lined spiral notebooks—and I thought I saved a few pennies with the value dozen pack. I told Jack that he had to squeeze his cursive letters in between the narrow lines because I'm too afraid to brave the mob of moms at Target again. Do you know a woman stole hole reinforcers right out of my shopping cart? The nerve! I refuse to set foot in that store anytime soon unless we're out of toilet paper.

Kosher Yoga: Mom's Best Friend

Finally, I discovered a healthy way to energize my body and calm my nerves. Best of all, this remedy for an overworked mom requires neither a shot of espresso nor a sedative. It's called Torah yoga and it's the ultimate "me" time. A good excuse to focus on myself for an hour, Torah yoga unites the mind, body, heart, and soul. Talk about multi-tasking.

The Torah has guided the Jewish people for thousands of years and uses traditional and mystical text to help us get closer to our true self and to God. Yoga is an ancient teaching as well, using breath and movement to find our inner spirit and higher power. Torah yoga is a combination of the western religion that emphasizes intellect and the eastern philosophy that considers the body our "temple." Now it all makes sense.

Come to think of it, I do feel closer to God when I roll onto my shoulders, point my legs toward my forehead, and think to myself, "If I don't get out of this pose soon I'm gonna die."

Actually, Torah yoga is not supposed to be uncomfortable, and the postures can be modified for any age or physical ability. Jewish yoga is considered kosher, which means fit to be used for ritual purposes. Fortunately, I don't have to bend my body in the shape of the Hebrew letter *Aleph* to enjoy the physical and emotional benefits, including stronger muscles, increased stamina, improved thyroid function, increased confidence, and relaxation. All it takes is an open mind to get started. Most of all, Jewish meditation requires me to be in the moment and breathe.

Our teacher, Maxine Mirowitz, wakes up before the sun to make the most of each day, which could include anything from running a marathon, backpacking in the Ozark mountains, lifting weights in the gym with her husband, planting flowers at the Missouri Botanical Gardens, or taking care of her turkey, pheasants, peacock, pigeons, koi fish, and parrots. Did I mention in her spare time that this avid cyclist also practices optometry?

In the Torah yoga class, Maxine has developed a series of classic yoga poses that flow together to warm the body and work the heart. With an inner and outward beauty, her big smile and bubbly personality make everyone feel at ease, not to mention she gracefully moves her body as if she's double jointed. She turns down the lights in the small chapel to prepare a dozen women for a one-hour spiritual and physical journey. The stained glass windows illuminate the room with the warm colors of red, blue, purple, and amber for a perfect serene setting.

We sit cross-legged on mats and towels as Maxine leads a 15-minute lesson on how *Sukkot* and yoga allow us to appreciate our abundance and how our bodies and nature work in harmony. Everyone participates in the discussion, which is based on a new topic every week from a Torah portion, Jewish holiday, or even a Buddhist teaching that inspires us to balance on one leg like a flamingo. With her bouncy, curly hair flowing over her shoulders, Maxine demonstrates and patiently explains the yoga poses, such as the downward dog, cobra, and bridge. One of the highlights of the class is when we sing the *Shema* in unison and each word is choreographed to a movement. At that moment I realize that it's not enough to read the Torah, I have to feel the prayers as well.

My other favorite part of the class is the final pose, known as the corpse. For this stress reliever, I lie on the floor and close my eyes. I temporarily forget about the to-do list in my head and focus instead on each inhale and exhale. I absorb the soothing sounds of classical guitar and chirping birds recorded in the Australian outback. I'm at peace for the moment. I hope nobody wakes me up anytime soon.

Why Moms Need To Be Fit

Moms these days are always on the run. We run errands. We run to the grocery store. We run after our children. We run around the house looking for misplaced math homework and lost car keys.

Moms are always on the go. We go to work and we go work out. We go to appointments and sometimes we go crazy. We go to baseball games and we go to soccer games. We go to birthday parties and we go to *bar mitzvahs*. We go shopping. Once in awhile, we go out to dinner. Sometimes we go too long and forget to go to the bathroom, but that's another story. I could go on and on.

Sure, we are running all the time, but are we healthy and in shape? In the olden days before gyms were invented, real exercise used to be part of everyday life for moms. Women got plenty of cardiovascular activity while they scrubbed the kitchen floor on their hands and knees, shoveled coal into the furnace, hung heavy wet sheets on the clothesline, tilled the soil in the garden, and walked everywhere because there were no cars.

Today, moms are busier than ever but not necessarily more active. That's why I joined a new health club down the street. I knew I was in for an adventure when I allowed a personal trainer named Chad to pinch my body fat in places that my own husband isn't allowed to go near.

A big selling point to this fitness center is that it's open 24 hours. Thanks to a workout facility that's available around the clock, I now can count calories instead of sheep in the middle of the night if I have insomnia. I no longer have an excuse not to exercise.

Like many exercise enthusiasts, I'm hooked on the elliptical machine. Finally, I get a total body workout without the stress on my creaking joints and bones. Sure, I go nowhere fast, but the built-in fan keeps me cool and comfortable. After all, comfort is key when I exercise. With a white terry cloth towel around my neck and a pink water bottle in my hand, I hop from the elliptical to the rower. I avoid any sporting device that looks painful, such as the stair climber, which reminds me why the escalator was invented.

Since multi-tasking is proven to increase metabolism, I power walk on the treadmill while I watch the news and my favorite talk show simultaneously on multiple television screens. Besides, exercise is more fun when I'm distracted. In the spinning studio, for example, I peddle my stationary bike as fast as I can and engross myself in the Tour de France movie projected on the wall. Yes, it's intimidating to be in the same room with real cyclists who aren't afraid to wear padded shorts in public, but I'm too embarrassed to sneak out of the class early and hit the hot tub.

Moms should make it a priority to take better care of their bodies. Especially since, typically, women live longer than men, we need to lead a good example of a healthy lifestyle for our children's sake. As I see it, an expensive gym membership is in the best interest of my family. Sure, I get plenty of exercise (and fresh air) when I jump on the trampoline with my kids, jog around the neighborhood, and ride my bike on nature trails, which doesn't cost a thing. Then again, neither does mowing the grass.

The Gallbladder Vacation

Sometimes moms go to extreme measures to get a little down time for themselves. Recently I figured out how to indulge in almost a full week of pampering without leaving the comfort of my own couch. All it took was the surgical removal of an organ. Luckily, I can live without my gallbladder.

Even though gallstones are the most common digestive disease in the United States and affect more than 20 million Americans with a million new cases diagnosed each year, many moms are clueless when it comes to the ambiguous, pear-shaped organ that sits beneath the liver in the right-upper abdomen. In case you're curious, the job of the gallbladder is to store bile, which is a digestive liquid continually secreted by the liver. The bile emulsifies fats and neutralizes acids in partly digested food. No wonder my gallbladder went kaput. I always eat too fast and rarely do I chew my food.

It turns out that one in 10 Americans suffers from gallbladder disease and females are up to four times as likely as males to develop gallstones due to multiple pregnancies, obesity, rapid weight loss, or heredity. Good thing women tolerate pain better than men.

At least my gallbladder attack is a good conversation starter, especially when every time I retell the story it gets more dramatic.

It all started about a month ago when I got out of bed in the middle of the night because I was restless and felt yucky or, in medical terms, malaise. So I paced the floor, trying to shake off the symptoms, which included tightness in my chest, nausea, heartburn, and arm stiffness. Naturally I went on the computer and Googled "heart attack symptoms for women." Never a good idea. I diagnosed myself with myocardial infarction and I had only two months to live.

I hurried back to our bedroom where Scott was snoring. I tried not to startle him when I whispered in his ear, "Either I'm having a heart attack or I ate too much frozen custard last night."

He jumped out of bed and called 911. Before I had a chance to revise my living will, the doorbell rang. There stood a nice-looking young man with a stethoscope around his neck. Even though I was hyperventilating into a paper bag, I managed to ask the paramedic if he was Jewish, single, and training to be a doctor. I figured that I needed to fulfill a *mitzvah* of arranging a marriage before I went to heaven.

Anyway, we sat on the living room couch and he asked me a few questions. For starters, "Have you ever experienced a panic attack or are you under any stress lately?" Despite the intensifying discomfort in my body, I barked at his insulting assumption.

"Stress? Ha! Have you ever planned a *bar mitzvah??!!*"

I was rushed to the emergency room where nurses immediately hooked me to wires and all sorts of beeping machines. An ultrasound revealed three miniscule gallstones. I bribed the resident doctor to let me stay overnight in the hospital for "observation" and free room service.

The next morning, my husband picked me up at Missouri Baptist Medical Center. The doctor on call advised me to eliminate fat from my diet (I suddenly craved a juicy cheeseburger) and told me to schedule an appointment with a surgeon as soon as possible. For souvenirs, I stashed the fuzzy slippers and giant insulated drinking cup in my purse.

Later that week I met with Dr. Zuke (pronounced zoo-kee), who explained how the gallbladder is like a squishy water balloon filled with teeny tiny marbles. In a common procedure known as laparoscopic cholecystectomy, Dr. Zuke would pull the gallbladder through a dime-sized hole cut inside my bellybutton.

I was given the choice of outpatient surgery or an overnight hospital stay. What a no brainer! I hurried back home and pulled my dusty suitcase out of the basement. I packed my toothbrush, a new pair of yellow and pink polka dot pajamas, and the book *Marley & Me.*

On the day of surgery, I checked into my beautiful suite and pretended that I was at a spa. The only difference was that this visit involved anesthesia. When I woke up in the recovery room after the one-hour procedure, I felt slightly disoriented. Was my mother really standing at the foot of my bed with a Tupperware container of *kamish* bread or was I delusional?

Every time I coughed, it felt like a sumo wrestler jumped on my stomach. Plus, nobody told me that the carbon dioxide used to inflate my abdomen during the operation caused serious shoulder and back pain. No big deal. Once the drugs kicked in again, I was oblivious and ready for a nap.

I was wheeled back into my beautiful private room with contemporary décor, hardwood floors, lots of big windows, and a flat screen television. I had a nurse all to myself and she served me as much yogurt, animal crackers, and narcotics as I wanted. She never complained when I buzzed her for assistance to use the bathroom. Together we awkwardly danced the tango with my IV tubes. To this day, I still dream about the mechanical bed that allowed me to perfectly balance my head and knees upright with the touch of a button. It takes at least seven pillows and a stack of encyclopedias to try to duplicate this ergonomic design in my own king-size bed at home.

I was in no hurry to leave the next morning. I wanted my full 24-hour vacation. So I called my husband and told him not to pick me up until check out time at noon. I ordered breakfast in bed—coffee and a giant chocolate muffin since they were fresh out of Eggs Benedict. As I rang the nurse for another pillow, my husband showed up. He was 45 minutes early.

"I'm not going anywhere yet," I insisted as I played some more with the buttons on the bed and maneuvered the lower half of my body. "Besides, I'm watching my favorite talk show, *The View*, and Barbara Walters is about to reveal her marital affairs."

But all good things must end, including the 24-hour gift given to me by my insurance company. I reluctantly dressed myself to go home, but I left my fuzzy socks with rubberized bottoms on my feet as a reminder that I was still worthy of sympathy from my husband and children. I said goodbye to the nurses (my new friends) and promised them that I'd be back one day for a facelift.

When I arrived home, I plopped down on the couch with everything I needed: pillows, blankets, magazines, saltines, water bottle, telephones, painkillers, remote controls, and my toy poodle Luci, who never left my lap.

While I continued to recover from surgery and regain my strength, I tried to take advantage of my time off. When I was tired, I lied down. The kids and I ate mint chocolate chip ice cream in front of the television and watched *American Idol*. I didn't sweat the small stuff. I didn't even make my bed. I left Jack's dirty socks on the floor because it hurt to bend over and pick them up.

Following doctor's orders, I avoided lifting anything heavy, such as a big pot of spaghetti, a laundry basket full of clothes, or grocery bags filled with canned soup. I walked around the house with my bloated belly hanging over my sweatpants as if I was in my third trimester of pregnancy. I just didn't care.

A week later at my follow-up appointment, the doctor removed my stitches and told me that I was almost ready to resume normal activity.

Maybe I should get a second opinion.

Obama Mamas And The Era Of Change

Where were you when Barack Obama placed his left hand on

Abraham Lincoln's burgundy velvet Bible and was sworn in as the 44th president of the United States?

The inauguration of 2009 was one of those defining moments in history, etched in some of our memories like the JFK assassination in 1963, the first walk on the moon in 1969, the Space Shuttle Challenger explosion in 1986, and the 9/11 terrorist attacks in 2001.

If you're a mom, chances are you were doing something else while you were glued to the most anticipated inauguration of our lifetime. I folded laundry on the couch as I watched history unfold. When Michelle Obama gave outgoing First Lady Laura Bush a white package wrapped in a red ribbon on the steps of the White House, I grabbed a box of Kleenex. When the adorable Sasha and Malia, dressed in J. Crew coats with ribbons, smiled at their dad, I smiled, too. When the chief justice of the Supreme Court fumbled over the words of the U.S. Constitution, I held my breath. When Aretha Franklin belted out "Let Freedom Ring!" and wore the biggest hat bow ever, I sang right along with the Queen of Soul. When the First Couple exited the "Beast" (their tank-like limo) and waved to the cheering record-breaking crowd that lined Pennsylvania Avenue, I was at the edge of my seat. And finally, when the Obamas danced at an Inaugural Ball later that night, I felt like I was watching a fairytale. When the President introduced his wife as the woman "who does everything I do, only backwards and in heels," my heart melted.

No doubt, the day that President Obama took the oath of office was unprecedented, and not just because the former Illinois senator was the first African American to become the leader of the free world and stand before the nation's Capitol that was originally built by slaves. The most widely watched televised event ever was remarkable for a multitude of reasons.

During his two-year campaign, the Ivy League grad and son of an African immigrant was able to mobilize the population, especially the social networking generation, to spread the word about patriotism, responsibility, and citizenship. His message was loud and clear when two million energetic people crowded the National Mall, braved the bitter cold, waved American flags, and enthusiastically chanted "O-Ba-Ma! O-Ba-Ma!"

Sure, the economy is in the toilet and the country is at war, but January 20, 2009 was a time to celebrate, a time to forget the divisions of race, religion, age, and partisanship.

For me, Obama's message reflects what the local Jewish community is all about—the frontrunners of change.

Moms On Facebook

I never thought that I was the type to crumble under peer pressure, surrender to the insanity, and plummet into the bizarre (to me) world of web-based social networking. Call me old fashioned, but I'd rather schmooze over a latte at Starbucks than kibbitz in cyberspace. Until recently, I associated Facebook and MySpace with bullying teenagers, child predators, and sly spouses about to break the Seventh Commandment.

Truth is, Facebook is serious fun for millions of people from all walks of life. Many are moms who want to build a community by connecting with old friends and making new ones with similar interests and activities. Facebook is a useful tool for moms in particular because we can monitor the mischievousness of our underage children and spy on their friends as well (if they'll "friend" us). We also can track down high school classmates who we haven't seen in decades, exchange cheese ball recipes, join the movement to support democracy in the Middle East, search for business opportunities, and send family vacation pictures to far away relatives. Not only that, we can get advice on everything from potty training and retirement planning to adoption and home schooling. Bottom line, Facebook brings people together.

This now $15 billion a year business is the brainchild of Mark Zuckerburg, who launched Facebook in 2004 from his dorm room at Harvard University. *Forbes* Magazine named Zuckerburg the world's youngest self-made billionaire. And he's Jewish.

The popularity of Facebook is undeniable. It now has more than 500 active million users, 70 percent of whom are outside the United States. It's available in more than 70 translations.

As if moms need another person to answer to, I already struggle to keep up with messages on my landline, cell phone, and emails. Now I have to check my Facebook page everyday. I need a secretary.

Not surprising, these online communities can be as addictive as chocolate-covered almonds. Once I get started I can't stop. Zuckerburg describes his invention as "contagious, infectious, and viral…but in a good way." Just think Webkinz, only for adults.

With so much emphasis on computerized communication and superficial relationships at an early age, the future generation is doomed to forget how to actually speak to real people and write complete sentences. Admittedly, since I became an official blogger, my own parental judgment seems impaired. The other night I was engrossed in Facebook, searching for a toy poodle fan club, and I didn't even notice that my daughter was watching flatulent monkey videos on a laptop computer right next to me. Not only that, it was way past her bedtime.

I'll never understand their idea of entertainment anyway. Lately when I drive my children in the car, they both insert their earplugs while I talk to myself. The silence is eerie. I miss the screaming.

Maybe that's why Facebook is so popular among moms. We feel like someone is actually listening to us. Of course, I rationalize my temporary obsession with Facebook as research for my column. And it's free. After all, if Barack Obama can launch his presidential campaign by drumming up support on Facebook, the least I can do is explore the possibilities for myself.

MommyBloggers Share The *Mishegas*

All these years I thought I had my act together as a mom. After all, my kids appear to be clean (so what's a little ear wax?), nourished (ketchup is a vegetable, right?), educated (thank goodness for spell check), and appropriately dressed (except for my son's plaid boxers hanging out of his baggy jeans).

At ages 12 and 15, neither Sari nor Jack has yet to flunk a class, swallow bubblegum, beat anybody up, get a tattoo (at least not that I know of), or been arrested for ding dong ditching in the neighborhood.

Somehow I've managed to pull this off while I make dinner, fold laundry, clean their retainers weekly with Efferdent, and schlep them to every sporting event, temple activity, and haircut appointment. Did I mention that I recycle and make banana bread from scratch?

Now I have another domestic duty to add to my parenting portfolio: blogging. That's right. It seems that everyone and their mother is a blogger these days. So much for my bachelor's degree in journalism. Even though I don't text, tweet, or operate the television remote control without assistance from my own children who roll their eyes at me every time I ask, "What does this button do?" I'm looking forward to schmoozing in cyberspace with fellow mommybloggers who try to keep their sanity while raising teenagers. It's cheaper than therapy.

With more than 36 million women writing and reading the 200,000-plus blogs on parenting and family, this growing phenomenon of female social networking is here to stay, especially among Jewish bloggers who are one of the biggest blogging groups out there. Whether you're a WOHM (work outside the home mom) or a WAHM (work at home mom), blogging is a perfect fit for us Jewish moms who tend to be intelligent, opinionated, outspoken, influential, and, let's face it, always looking for a distraction from emptying the dishwasher.

I've noticed that mommybloggers, who carry their laptops as purses, have their own lingo, too, like "mompreneur" (a professional mom), "momocrat" (a political-minded mom), "mamarazzi" (a celebrity-obsessed mom), "mombian" (a lesbian mom), "e-mom" (a mom with a home-based business), and "ecomom" (an environmentally friendly mom). They have "momversations" and "mommalogues" on their "vlogs," or video logs, thanks to YouTube.

The other day I was so engrossed in mommyblogs that I missed a mammogram appointment. Not only that, I'm pretty sure I have carpal tunnel syndrome from typing so much on my keyboard. On one blog, I shopped for a handcrafted glass *mezuzah*, watched a video on how to make the perfect matzo ball, brushed up on the blessing over the children, and listened to the latest Israeli hip hop music. Talk about multi-tasking!

Better Yourself Again In 2010

Once again, my New Year's Resolution is to never make another New Year's Resolution, and this time I'm sticking to it. I figure, why bother setting myself up for failure when any promise I make to shed a few pounds is usually broken before the Super Bowl playoffs anyway? As soon as I tell myself that I won't mindlessly munch on as many carbs, I start to fantasize about Mr. Salty Pretzel himself. Likewise, if I make a commitment to be a better parent, I feel even guiltier when I daydream about the laundry instead of paying attention to my daughter's drawn-out synopsis of gym class.

Still, for those of you who follow tradition to make a resolution or set a personal goal, then more power to you. To improve your chances of success, here's what the experts advise:

First, be realistic. Don't bite off more than you can chew (unless it's a cream-filled donut). Set short-term goals instead of long-term ones. For example, it seems easier to lose one pound a month than 20 pounds in a year. Also, be specific and choose only one or two goals so that you won't feel overwhelmed and will have a better chance of scratching something off your list. If you aim for the same resolution year after year and don't get anywhere, accept your thick waistline as a genetic mishap and move onto something else.

Next, write down your resolution(s) and post them on your bathroom mirror or refrigerator so that you can get a daily, visual reminder of what's important to you. On the same note, tell your spouse or friend or a co-worker about your plans, so that they can offer support or harass you.

Finally, reward yourself for each milestone. Whether you go to a movie, try a new restaurant, or get a massage, you'll stay motivated to work toward your goal. Even if your focus is to lose weight, it won't hurt to splurge on a hot fudge sundae once in awhile so that you don't feel deprived.

So, what does Judaism tell us about our obsession to change ourselves? The early Hassidic sage Rabbi Zusya said, "When I reach the next world, God will not ask me, 'Why were you not Moses.' Instead, he will ask me, 'Why were you not Zusya?'"

In other words, the best we can do is *be* the person we were meant to be and not who we are perceived to be in the eyes of others. In order for that deep thought to sink in, I need a bite of cheesecake. Have a happy, healthy, and honest-with-yourself New Year!

Get Real Resolutions

Want to improve the quality of your life this year? First, pop the cork on that bottle of Asti Spumante that has been in the refrigerator behind the stale box of baking soda since you got married in 1993. After you make a toast, pour the bubbly down the drain because it's probably flat and tastes like water.

Second, never stop learning. It's never too late to learn something new or start a hobby. Whether you take a scuba diving class, knit a scarf, make challah, speak Hebrew, read *The Great Gatsby*, make a book out of favorite family recipes, collect coins or stamps, hike the red granite Sinai mountains in Israel, or start training for a half marathon, you'll add a new dimension to your world when you actively use your brain and body.

Third, remember it's not about you. *Mitzvahs* are trendy during the holiday season, but volunteerism is a way of life all year round. A few ways to help in the community on a regular basis with your family include stocking canned goods at the food pantry, exercising dogs at the Humane Society, participating in a community project at your temple, delivering hot dinners to the homebound, planting a tree in a park, or coming up with your own special way to give back, something that really touches your heart, like teaching the teenagers in your neighborhood how to parallel park their cars away from your driveway.

Fourth, clean up your act. Once you start organizing your stuff you can't stop. Start with something easy—your sock drawer. Next, move on to your wardrobe closet where there're probably clothes that you haven't worn since your honeymoon. While you're on a roll, clean out your medicine cabinet and straighten up your spice rack. Also, unless your kids are still using empty cardboard boxes in the basement to build forts, it's time to recycle them (the boxes, not your children). Finally, put scattered photos in an album or scrapbook before your great grandchildren get stuck with the job after you're dead.

Fifth, escape your comfort zone. For a youngster, it might mean trying Brussels sprouts for the first time. For an adult, it can be changing career paths or resolving a conflict with a loved one by making the first phone call. Taking risks leads to rewards, whether it's stretching in a Pilates class, striking up a conversation with someone you don't know, or sending a manuscript to a publisher. Show your kids that success in life doesn't come without failures; it's a philosophy we never outgrow.

Sixth, listen more and talk less. The old adage about one mouth and two ears is generally true, but don't ask me where I heard this or what it means. Basically, I think it means to listen twice as much as you talk. For parents, it means to listen better to what their kids are saying; they may want a sounding board, not advice or problem solving. By doing so, we may empower them to solve their own problems. In the words of Stephen Covey, "Seek first to understand, then to be understood." Not sure what that means either, but it sounds good.

Finally, lighten up. Don't take life so seriously, and don't sweat the small stuff. When striving for success, don't get bogged down with the details, because it's all in the journey, not the destination. When was the last time you had a good belly laugh? Laughter actually relieves stress, loosens muscles, lowers blood pressure, and may lower levels of hormones that create stress and weaken immunity. When you laugh, your body moves blood to your heart and lungs, boosting your energy level and making you feel better instantly.

And that beats exercise.

My Secret Obsession

I'm obsessed with the Food Network. My favorites include anything with the adorably perky Rachael Ray, who makes every 30-minute meal look like a no-brainer. Plus, I'm amazed at how her long, floppy brown hair never dips into the spaghetti sauce. I also indulge in the silver-haired southerner Paula Deen because she brings class to comfort food. The friendly country cook also has a serious sweet tooth and isn't afraid to use real butter. I'll never forget how in one episode, she declared, "This mulled apple cider is so easy, ya'll, it's stupid." Now that's my kind of recipe!

I admit that I'm kind of intimidated by the gorgeous Italian chef Giada De Laurentiis, who has the tiniest waist, biggest smile, and whitest teeth ever. To keep her girlish figure, I'm convinced that she spits out the baked ziti during commercials. Moreover, she never seems to break a sweat, not even under intense pressure at Iron Chef competitions. Speaking of beautiful, I'm also hooked on the impeccably dressed Sandra Lee, who I call Sandra Dee because she plays an All-American goody two-shoes even as she mixes another cocktail. To give you an idea of her perfection, her flawless makeup and fashionable outfits always coordinate with the color of her ever-changing kitchen décor, right down to the lavender dishtowels.

Finally, hunks like Michael Chiarello make it macho to toss a Caesar salad. When the master of easy entertaining wears a kiwi-colored shirt, he's as inviting as a spring day. Likewise, guy-next-door Tyler Florence really knows how to heat up the kitchen. The other day he and an Israeli guest deep-fried the crispiest and tastiest looking falafels I've ever seen. On the other hand, Emeril's giblet gravy does nothing for me. Sorry.

It's no wonder that my daughter has inherited my fetish to watch the 24-hour cooking channel. In fact, Sari idolizes Rachael Ray. I'm serious. Every time I heat the skillet, Sari asks me, "Mom, are you using E.V.O.O.?"

I sometimes like to pretend that I have my own cooking show in the privacy of my kitchen. That's right, while I make banana chocolate chip muffins or zesty chicken spiral noodle casserole, I demonstrate to an imaginary audience how I pack down brown sugar or enthusiastically karate chop a red pepper.

I've learned some valuable lessons from my Food Network obsession. First, I try to remember to read the entire recipe before I get started, otherwise I get to the end and realize I was supposed to sprinkle the mozzarella on top during the last five minutes of baking. Another rule is to make sure I have all the ingredients before I crack the first egg. One time I was midway into the batter of chocolate espresso brownies when I discovered that I had no espresso powder and no bittersweet chocolate. And sometimes I forget that I have oatmeal cookies in the oven until

I smell something burning. I hate when that happens.

And that brings me to another point. Why aren't there any Jewish cooking shows? Is it because no *baleboostehs* want to share their brisket recipes? Maybe it's because viewers don't want to clog their arteries with chopped liver and kreplach. Mediterranean fair, such as hummus and tabouleh, are hip these days, so I'm sure I'm onto something. Maybe if I keep practicing my techniques on chopping parsley, I will one day feel confident enough to pitch my own reality cooking show, called, "Mommmm, what's for dinner??!!!"

Forgive Me, For I Have Sinned

Typically, Jews don't make confessions. Instead we carry our guilt like heavy bricks on our backs the way our ancestors did when they were slaves in Egypt.

To relieve my burden, I've written my confessions here. For example, I seek forgiveness when I:

• Curse my children while I photograph them for our annual holiday card, especially if they aren't smiling the right way or look like they don't love each other.

• Permit my children to eat only the end pieces of *kamish* bread, while I save the perfectly shaped cookies for company.

• Tear out recipes in magazines that are the property of the dentist's office.

• Serve white bread when I know whole wheat has all the nutrition and fiber.

• Cry every time I read anything from "Chicken Soup for the

Soul" books or listen to the "Yentl" soundtrack.

• Prohibit my teenage son from growing up because I still peel the apple skins and cut the bruises off bananas for him.

• Throw a towel in the dirty laundry after every shower even though I know it's clean and running the washing machine non-stop is bad for the environment.

• Make my daughter sleep on the floor in my bedroom when my dog is in bed with me nestled on a silk pillow and down comforter.

• Participate in book club for the wine and camaraderie when I only read the inside cover.

• Still don't know how to operate the television remote control without the help of my children.

• Don't decalcify my coffeepot with vinegar every three months.

• Borrow coins from the family *tzedakah* jar to pay for Girl Scout cookies.

• Eat a bagel during the week of Passover.

• Throw away SAT scores, report cards, and ribbons from assorted relay races instead of keeping them in scrapbooks.

• Use triple the amount of blackberry wine as the *charoset* recipe calls for so that my kids sleep soundly at night.

• Pretend that free samples of food at the grocery store have no calories.

• Wear PajamaJeans.

Roaring About Tiger Mom

The controversial book *Battle Hymn of the Tiger Mother* has many moms in an uproar. The author under attack is Amy Chua, a professor at Yale University Law School. In her book she is critical of what she sees as permissive American parenting and claims that Chinese mothers are superior to Western parents. Ironically this first generation Chinese-American is married to fellow Yale law professor Jed Rubenfeld and they are raising their two daughters, now teenagers, as Jews.

We've all heard the horror stories about this draconian mom. For starters, she prohibits play dates and sleepovers. Can you imagine? My daughter lives for getting together with her friends on the weekends. And, frankly, so do I, as long as they stay up all night, paint their fingernails, and crumble popcorn on the carpet at someone else's house.

Chua uses extreme parenting tactics to coerce her children into doing what she wants. If my kids take their dishes to the sink without me asking, I feel like I owe them Dairy Queen for dessert. Chua, on the other hand, doesn't think twice about insulting her own flesh and blood. On occasion, she has admitted to calling them "garbage" and "fat" and "lazy" and "stupid." Then again, she also has burned their stuffed animals and prohibited bathroom and water breaks until all studying is done. If I yell to my kids, "Clean your room—it looks like a pigsty," I'm convinced they'll wind up in therapy years down the road.

Chua writes, "To be a 'Chinese' parent, you have to be hated sometimes by someone you love and who hopefully loves you, and there's just no letting up, no point at which it suddenly becomes easy."

Her husband must be a mama's boy if he lets his wife get away with this mental abuse. Sure, Americans spoil their kids and go overboard on self-esteem when even the players on the last place little league team have to get a trophy so that nobody cries, including the parents. Still, I have a real problem with Chua's philosophy of measuring success by perfection, and so do the experts.

In particular, "There is a terrible epidemic of perfectionism in American girls," notes Wendy Mogel, author of my absolute favorite parenting manual, *The Blessing of a Skinned Knee: Using Jewish Teachings to Raise Self-Reliant Children* (which has been translated into Mandarin and Korean). "Anxiety about being physically perfect and academically accomplished has triggered eating disorders and other destructive behaviors in many teenage girls," adds Mogel, whose newest title *The Blessing of a B Minus: Using Jewish Teachings to Raise Resilient Teenagers* is also on my bookshelf.

Don't get me wrong. Education is a top priority, and college graduation is the norm rather than the exception in most Jewish families. However, parents should encourage their children to be street smart as well as book smart. Common sense goes a long way in the real world. The way I see it, some American students might fall short in standardized test scores, but others may lead the way in the true spirit of entrepreneurship.

In other words, the lessons that youngsters learn outside the classroom, whether they play a team sport or get involved in their temple youth group, is what really makes the grade. Children need to identify their special skills and interests, get along with other people, make wise choices, and, most importantly, learn from mistakes. On top of that, Jewish holidays and traditions teach young people the values and morals they need to achieve a successful, happy, and meaningful life.

Personally, I take more pride when my daughter gets a

compliment about her behavior than I do about her being in the gifted program. Besides, in my opinion, Jewish guilt is much more effective in child rearing than the Chinese way Chua proclaims in her book.

For example, when my son would rather watch YouTube videos than do his homework, I can say, "Fine. Don't finish your essay on the Industrial Revolution. What do I care if my only son doesn't get a job out of college and has to live with his mother for the rest of his life."

That should motivate him to hit the books.

Women Celebrate Their Inner Curl

If beauty is only skin deep, then why do women fuss so much over their hair? If our hair is straight, we curl it with a perm. If our hair is curly, we straighten it with a flat iron. In my opinion, having a bad hair day merits a good excuse to crawl back in bed.

For generations, women have gone to great lengths to preserve their hairdos. Certainly the accumulated fumes of hairspray have permanently damaged the ozone layer. My own mother, for example, used to zip a nylon hood over her face so that her coiffure wouldn't get messed up when she got dressed.

Hair has deep roots in Jewish history. In fact, lovely locks inspired poetry in the Biblical Song of Songs with "Your hair is like a flock of goats from Gilead." The Talmud regarded woman's hair as beautiful and erotic and for that reason it had to be covered.

Beauty is symbolic in Judaism, going back to Sarah, Rebecca, Rachel, and Leah. These archetypes of Jewish womanhood were singled out for their attractiveness. Sarah is "a woman of beautiful appearance" (Genesis 12:11); Rebecca is "very fair to look upon" (Genesis 24:16); Rachel is "beautiful of form and beautiful of appearance" and Leah's "eyes were tender" (Genesis 29:17).

Although the focus here is on outward appearance, the Bible implies that physical beauty is a metaphor for inner beauty because these women are revered not as much for their looks as they are for their goodness.

Perhaps no other woman epitomizes both inner and outward beauty more than Queen Esther, according to the *Megillah*, the story of Purim. Her exquisite beauty, grace, and poise set her apart from all the other maidens in Persia. In addition to physical beauty, Queen Esther possessed inner beauty through courage, confidence, obedience, honesty, self-sacrifice, wisdom, and a devotion to God. She saved the Jewish people from near-certain slaughter, and for this she was a true heroine.

On Purim, we celebrate the victory of the Jews and honor the beautiful Queen Esther by letting our hair down, literally, whether it's thick, fine, curly, straight, or somewhere in between. In addition to a jubilant party with wild costumes and noisy *graggers*, Purim gives Jewish women an opportunity to discover their inner and outer beauty in Queen Esther style. The lesson of Purim is to rejoice in our uniqueness and treat ourselves like queens.

Here's a popular rhyme about Queen Esther:

I need a queen, a nice new queen
To sit beside me on my throne.
And if she's very nice to me
I'll give her half of all I own.

This silly rhyme is a favorite Purim song among preschoolers, who parade in their gowns, crowns, and swords every year on the fourteenth day of *Adar* and pretend to be powerful King Ahasuerus, villainous Haman, blessed Mordecai, and his younger cousin, the beautiful Queen Esther.

On this mysterious and mischievous holiday, children aren't the only ones who shake their *groggers* and have a great time. Jews of all ages are invited to act out the characters in the Book of Esther. To celebrate the deliverance of the Jews of Persia with "days of feasting and gladness," grownups are encouraged to dress in masks and crazy costumes and drink plenty of spirits to the point where they can't tell the difference between good (*Mordecai*) and evil (*Haman*). Now that's what I call the whole *megillah*!

Since so much of Jewish thought is based on personal interpretations, it's possible that God created Queen Esther to inspire women and mothers in the future. Like Esther, a woman must hold her head high and not be afraid to use her beauty, strength, intelligence, and charm to make a difference in the world. Like Esther, who faces her fears and makes sacrifices for the sake of the Persian Jewry, a mother always puts her family first and does whatever it takes to protect her children from harm.

Like Esther, whose natural beauty wins over the heart of the king, a wise woman learns to accept her own inner and outer qualities. Like Esther, a confident woman realizes that what you see is what you get. Even though Esther hid her true identity as a Jew at first, her deception had a purpose: the survival of her people.

Like Esther, who risks her life as she bravely approaches the King without being summoned, a woman must risk failure to achieve success and she must always seek the truth. In addition, Esther uses her gentle nature to persuade the King to grant her anything she wants, including another decree for the Jews to protect themselves if they're attacked. Likewise, a woman realizes the power of kindness when it comes to earning love, respect, and trust of others.

Like Esther, who prays and fasts for three days before she squeezes into her royal robes and hosts a special feast to expose Haman's cruel plans, a typical woman usually diets before any big event.

Some things, I guess, never change.

Helping Children Cope Gives Us Hope

The morning starts out innocent enough. Like every other school day, Sari brushes her sun-streaked curls before I twirl her soft hair into a ponytail. She checks her homework while I whip up a strawberry yogurt smoothie for us to share at breakfast. I join Sari at the kitchen table and watch her use one finger to carefully spread cream cheese on a blueberry bagel. Then, out of nowhere, she asks me, "Has Osama Bin Laden been caught yet?"

The school bell across the street is about to ring and my daughter wants to discuss the latest conflict in the Middle East. "The bad guy is still hiding in a cave," I tell her. "Now go brush your teeth."

As I rinse the dishes in the sink, I realize that this particular Monday morning is not so innocent after all. Like so many other young people, Sari is no longer oblivious to the violence in our world. On this sunshiny day, we hold hands and cross the street to the school. Meanwhile, hundreds of children in war-ravaged cities like Haifa and Tyre, in southern Lebanon, flee to crowded bomb shelters.

Many parents, including me, struggle with how to talk to our children about war and terrorism. Since I don't fully understand the deep history and complicated politics myself, the dialogue is even more difficult. There're no easy answers, but one thing I know for sure. All of us want to feel safe. The best way for me to help Sari and Jack feel safe is to listen to their fears and concerns. I try to keep our discussions simple. I reassure them that the war is far away and they are safe at home. Even though I'm aware of news reports that warn us everyday of new threats to our homeland, I tell them that the president's job is to protect our country. We talk about how most people are good and just a few are led astray by evil leaders. Finally, I reinforce what they learn in Sunday school—we are the "chosen people." Jews are small but mighty. And, unlike any other country, Israel has stood strong and survived many, many battles for thousands of years.

Sometimes I get stuck on a sensitive topic that hits close to home, such as this one:

Sari: "Why can't we carry liquids, like baby shampoo or a juice box, on the airplane when we fly to Florida anymore?"
Me: "Ummmm…Airline passengers have to carry on less baggage these days to help save fuel."
Jack: "That's not what I heard. We aren't allowed to bring even cough medicine on the airplane because the terrorists have tried to make bombs and kill people."
Sari: "Is that true mom?"
Me: "The airport police work very hard to check everyone's bags and protect us from danger."
Sari: "That's good. Because I really want to go to the beach."

So the leisurely days of travel are bygone memories. I remember when I flew on an airplane as a child, my mother's biggest concern was to prevent me from throwing up. In fact, I never left the ground without melting a pasty Dramamine on my tongue. Nowadays, our generation of parents worries about weapons, not just motion sickness, when the 747 leaves the runway.

The airline industry reflects how the world is changing. The warfront once again invades our homes through the Internet, television, radio, and countless magazine and newspaper covers that glare at our children in the supermarket checkout lines next to the Snickers. Whenever possible, I exercise parental control and try to shield them from too much scary stuff. For example, when we're together I try not to watch the television news. Graphic scenes of demolished neighborhoods, bloody civilians, rows of body bags, blaring ambulance sirens, and explosive Katyusha rockets trigger nightmares for children and adults.

During wartime or any crisis situation, whether it's a natural catastrophe like an earthquake or a man-made disaster like the 9/11 attacks, parents need tools to handle their children's emotional well-being. As far as the war in Israel, the best defense against ignorance is education. When Sari asks me, "What's the Gaza Strip?" I want to know where and what she's talking about. That's why I try to stay up-to-date on the latest developments. With adult supervision, the Internet is an excellent way for children to stay informed. One of my favorite age-appropriate websites is www.babaganewz.com.

In times of uncertainty, children need their parents more than ever. The easiest way to help our children is to spend a little extra time with each other. If they are confused or anxious, give them something to do, such as draw pictures and write stories to express their feelings. They can also make cards for families of fallen soldiers and civilians killed.

I also set a good example for my children when I stand behind Israel and show my support, whether it's a donation to the Israel Emergency Campaign or participation in the local Jewish community's efforts to help the growing number of displaced families in Israel. Although we don't have family or friends in Israel right now, we're still one big family.

Finally, we can include Israel in our daily prayers. The Torah prophesizes that "the Jews over time will be scattered among nations…and will always be few in number." Our prophets wrote that Jews are a "light unto nations." With these powerful words, we can teach our children about our history and that hope is eternal.

For WAHMs, It's Business UNusual

People ask me all the time, "Ellie, how do you work from home with so many distractions during the day?" The answer is simple. I'd much rather stay home and write in my flannel pajamas than get dressed in real clothes and drive to an office where I would doodle pictures at boring meetings and sit at my desk during my one-hour lunch break and eat leftover meatloaf out of a Tupperware container.

I consider myself lucky that I'm able to work from home, especially while Jack and Sari still look forward to seeing my smiling face when they get home from school. As a freelance writer for the past 25 years, my flexible schedule allows me to be at my family's beck and call. On the flip side, it's impossible for me to leave my work at the office and I always feel like I have an unfinished project hanging over my head.

For many moms who work at home, business as usual takes on a whole new meaning. Sometimes my domestic responsibilities overlap with my professional ones, and since I don't have the luxury of a private conference room, I've had to make the best of some sticky situations. For example, over the years, I've negotiated with editors and conducted interviews for stories while I trimmed fat off raw chicken, changed diapers, and folded laundry. I've locked myself in the bathroom so that the person on the other end didn't hear my child screaming at me. One time, I even had to interrupt a photo shoot in my own kitchen because Luci ran down the street and nobody would chase after her. For me, it's all in a day's work. If I have to stay up later than Conan O'Brien to meet a deadline, oh well, at least I can crank out copy while I wear my bathrobe and slippers instead of pantyhose and pumps.

Moms want the best of both worlds. We want our careers and we crave our freedom. In order to capitalize on our special talents and interests, let's face it, we need a little discipline and a lot of Dove chocolate. This rule applies to any occupation, whether we sell Arbonne anti-aging cream, design crystal jewelry, write a newspaper column, provide financial consultations, or build websites from our home headquarters. For those work-at-home moms who are serious about getting the job done, here are a few survival tips to consider:

1. Create a workspace that is comfortable and convenient, whether your office is located in the unfinished basement, spare bedroom, or empty formal living room that no one has stepped foot in since the Little Tykes playhouse was disassembled and donated to charity.

2. If you share a computer with your kids, make sure that they know who's the boss. And, hopefully, they will give you a turn after they place their final bid on an Albert Pujoles baseball card on eBay. Also, beware of dangerous Disney computer games that can corrupt your important files just when you need them most.

3. Keep all your essential supplies handy. In my desk drawer, for example, I have plenty of sticky note pads, assorted paper clips, dried out highlighters, unsharpened pencils, an empty roll of Scotch tape, stale gum, tape measure, calculator, stapler, and dull emery board that I use when I have writer's block.

4. Get plenty of exercise. This includes repetitive sprints to the freezer for another scoop of Cherry Garcia ice cream.

5. Frequently monitor the mailbox, especially when you've

been promised, "Your check is in the mail."

6. If the weather is nice, walk your dog, who has been a warm, fuzzy ottoman at your feet. If you don't have a dog, offer to walk your neighbor's dog and you'll never feel guilty about borrowing a box of Minute Rice again.

7. Don't sit too long in a desk chair, unless you're doing regular kegel exercises and leg lifts with weights strapped to your ankles.

8. Keep up with the housework. Every time you pass something that looks dusty, wipe it with the sleeve of your sweatshirt.

9. Take frequent breaks that are scheduled around your favorite celebrity appearances on *The Ellen DeGeneres Show* and *E! True Hollywood Story*.

10. Stock the pantry with s'mores ingredients at all times because you never know when you'll want to build a campfire or just grab a piece of emergency chocolate.

11. When the phone rings, don't answer it, unless it's your mother or the school nurse. If you're in deep thought or on a roll, the last thing you need are interruptions from solicitors or your husband wanting to know what's for dinner.

12. Finally, to get the creative juices flowing, go shopping.

Making Conversation With Answering Machines

Let's face it—we live in a world of faceless communication. Answering machines and other wireless wizardry substitute real voices, not to mention impersonal e-mails take the place of handwritten letters. Think about it–phone tag is now considered a sport or human interaction, and I'm guilty of playing the game. As a matter of fact, if I call someone's number and a real person answers the phone, I'm disappointed because I'm not in the mood to make real conversation anymore. That's why I like to call people in the middle of the day when no one is usually home. I get by with a message that's short and sweet: "Hey, it's Ellie. Please bring a bag of pretzels for the school party tomorrow. Thanks! Bye!"

My answering machine is my best ally. For example, when I don't want to talk to a solicitor, I let my answering machine do the dirty work for me. When the phone rings in the middle of dinner, my answering machine screens my calls and lets me decide when I want to talk and to whom. My husband actually programmed different ring tones to identify frequent callers. If we hear church bells, it's Grandma Ruth. If we hear a croaking frog, it's Uncle Kevin.

The answering machine is also a reliable friend. When I come home after a long day of running errands, the red flashing light greets me without fail. One friend is so comfortable with answering machines that she regularly has lengthy conversations with herself, only for me to endure later when I hit the play button. In fact, in the time it takes her to say her *schpiel*, I'll empty the dishwasher, boil spaghetti, and fold a load of towels before I eventually hear a beep. I don't mind long messages because I feel like we catch up with each other that way. Besides, nothing insults me more than an answering machine that hangs up before I do.

Nowadays, everyone wants immediate gratification and convenience, and each generation wants a faster and easier way to reach people. For me, answering machines and e-mails are necessary evils. I've become so lazy that I e-mail my neighbor across the street instead of knocking on her door. And the best way to get my husband's attention is to e-mail him at work.

The other day, I discovered something rare in my mailbox. In the pile of catalogs and bank applications was a lovely, ivory-colored note card with my full name handwritten on the matching monogrammed envelope. I could tell this letter was something special, so I carefully examined the foreign object before I even read a cursive word. The old-fashioned fringed edges reminded me of a lost piece of correspondence that my mother might have written long ago. I felt as if this piece of paper was a treasure that belonged in a glass display case at the museum of sociology.

It was comforting to read something that wasn't typed on a computer or abbreviated for a change. Turns out that a charming lady from the Lights of the Jewish Special Needs wrote me this letter, graciously inviting me to speak at the organization's annual spring luncheon. Needless to say, I wanted to respond to her flattering offer right away. Fortunately, she wrote her phone number and e-mail on the bottom of the page. Since this grandmother-on-the-go wasn't home, I left a message on her answering machine.

Lice Liven Up Seder But Traumatize Household

When it comes to the 10 plagues in the Passover story, I'd rather suffer in real life through a hailstorm (I've got insurance) and darkness (I'll carry a flashlight) than go through the anguish of lice again. These pesky little insects are a parent's worst nightmare. Just ask me. I lived through lice three years ago when my daughter and several of her unlucky classmates got the itch to scratch while they were still in preschool.

I remember the day that lice turned my happy home upside down.

As Sari sat on my lap at the pediatrician's office for a regular check-up, I noticed a grayish bug, barely the size of a sesame seed, crawling along the crooked part of her braided pigtails.

I didn't want to alarm Sari, so I quietly pointed out my finding to the doctor, who confirmed my biggest fear. "Yep, that's lice!" she blurted out. Sari jumped off my lap, or maybe I pushed her, as the doctor hurriedly prescribed a medicated shampoo and abruptly escorted us out of the exam room without a lollipop.

I lost count of the number of red lights that I drove through as we rushed to the nearest Walgreens. Sari was scared and cried the whole way. I tried to calm her down, but I, too, was plenty worried. I was petrified that a clawed, parasitic creature was sucking my baby's blood like a vampire and then defecating wherever it wanted. Even worse, I was grossed out that lice glued their nits, or eggs, to my daughter's gorgeous, shiny hair that used to smell like orange mango shampoo. I started to panic when I imagined that this highly contagious insect had the tenacity to potentially invade our cars, home, clothes, carpet, stuffed animals, blankets, and everything else that Sari came in contact with, including her own family and friends.

When we finally got to the store, I grabbed Sari's hand and dragged her up and down the aisles as we looked for the most effective lice killer. Even though I knew better than to attach a social stigma to lice, I still was embarrassed that someone would notice us. Now I understood what my husband felt like when he once bought me sanitary napkins, only this experience was a million times worse. I was paranoid that another customer would think we were homeless and never bathed.

I wanted to escape the drugstore as soon as possible so that I could get home and take care of my insect-infested child. Unfortunately, I was so overwhelmed with all the different brands and strengths of over-the-counter shampoos and conditioners that we hung out for hours like we were shopping for school supplies.

Finally, we made a decision and bought what we thought we needed, including gummy bears and an extra large chocolate bar. We wasted no time when we got home. I threw away Sari's Hello Kitty backpack (she never liked it anyway) and washed her coat and clothes in boiling hot water. The washing machine and dryer never stopped. I laundered everything that could be contaminated, including towels, sheets, blankets, pillows, and clothing. I suffocated all her stuffed animals in trash bags and tossed them in the dark basement. I disposed of her brushes, combs, and her collection of hair accessories. It was a traumatic day.

Next, I threw Sari in the shower and tried to make sense of the tiny print on the shampoo instructions that might as well have been written in Chinese. I felt like an exhausted and confused first-time mom, who attempted to calculate the right amounts of liquid and formula powder in the middle of another sleepless night. The directions mentioned something about harmful pesticides... flammable ingredients... burning scalp...and use caution if you have allergies, asthma, or pets...Huh?

Even though I was unsure of the possible side effects, I massaged the doctor-recommended, anti-lice shampoo in Sari's scalp and hair anyway. I told her to leave the stinky stuff in her hair for at least 10 minutes and reminded her not to breathe deeply or, God forbid, get the poison in her eyes and go blind. I never mentioned that she had to repeat the treatment in a week to kill any newly hatched lice.

Little did I know that the torture had only begun. After I rinsed and towel dried her tangles, I discovered the true meaning of nit picking. I rubbed nit removal gel in her thick mane and, with a special plastic comb, painstakingly raked through each strand of hair until I was dizzy from squinting my eyes so much. I felt like a demented scientist with a magnifying glass and 100-watt bulb. I was on a mission to extract any lice or nits, which were as small as a spec of salt and comparable to a needle in a haystack. If I found something that looked suspicious, I didn't take any chances. I carefully singled out each hair and cut the strand with scissors. Then I sealed the six-legged specimen in a plastic sandwich bag and watched it slowly die.

For the next several days, Sari was under quarantine like she had the chicken pox. She stayed home from school and didn't play with her pals. I wouldn't let her sit on the upholstered furniture, so she stood a lot. Whenever she scratched her head, I grabbed my nit comb and scissors. She was almost bald.

To contain an outbreak, I vacuumed constantly. The carpet and sofa never looked cleaner. I begged my husband for hardwood floors or at least a new vacuum. It never happened. He replaced the bag in the vacuum instead. Like a mad woman, I dragged the heavy Hoover into the garage and sucked up every crumb in the seat cushions and floor of the van.

Everything appeared tidy, but I was frustrated and tired of cleaning all the time. This tiny insect brought me to my knees. I left like one of Pharaoh's slaves. A few days after the first treatment, I found another nit in Sari's hair. I called the doctor and begged for help. The nurse asked me if I tried olive oil and vinegar. "I'm not looking for a recipe," I snapped at her. "I want a serious weapon to destroy the enemy."

But as crazy as it sounded, I was willing to try anything to get my normal life back again. I felt sorry for Sari, so I shared her misery. Together, we drenched our heads in olive oil. We tucked our greasy hair under plastic shower caps and wiped whatever mess oozed into our ears. We somehow managed to sleep in our silly bonnets most of the night. Early the next morning, we rinsed our hair with distilled vinegar. Surprisingly, our hair was more manageable and softer than ever.

We remember our days of suffering every year at the Passover seder, and when Sari acts out the 10 plagues, the closest she comes to lice is when she shakes a bag of dried rice.

Amen.

When It Comes To My Memory, Forget About it

Motherhood changes a woman in so many ways that she's never the same person again. Something happens during the birthing process that not only warps her cognitive skills but messes with the nerve cells that control memory and the ability to focus on one thing at a time. No wonder moms share a common characteristic: forgetfulness. The frequency of these amnesia-like attacks increases over the years, in much the same way that the mismatched assortment of plastic drinking cups and lids with chewed straws accumulate over time.

Otherwise, how else can I explain why I repeatedly call family members by their wrong names, including my dog Luci, until I get it right? There's only one explanation for such bizarre behavior: motherhood. Many moms share this embarrassing predicament. We forget our destinations while we drive our cars. We walk into a room to get something and our minds go blank. Sure, there's a purpose for our actions, but we just can't recall what it is.

For me, my short-term memory is the worst. That's why I can never find my car keys. Before I became a mom, I rarely lost my keys. Now my keys disappear right before my eyes. I have the same problem with other accessories, including my cell phone, driver's license, insurance card, sunglasses, and coupons for car washes, not to mention umbrellas and fruit-flavored ChapSticks. Once I even mistook a pack of Trident for my rectangular remote clicker at the bottom of my tote and consequently locked the keys inside my van. Thankfully, the engine wasn't running, at least not that time.

I misplace my keys at least three times in a 24-hour period, depending on the weather, my outfit, and the day of the week. How can I possibly keep track of my keys when I change my jacket, purse, gym bag, and vehicle more often than my son switches television channels?

Most husbands, including mine, can't relate to their wife's dilemma. Scott keeps his keys and wallet inside what appears to be a bottomless pocket of his faded Levi's. For the most part, he empties his stash in a basket that I've conveniently placed right inside the laundry room door. Sounds like a logical way for me to organize my stuff as well, but for some reason my keys never seem to find their way in the handy container.

Instead, my keys end up in the strangest places. My keys are known to dangle from a doorknob, hide inside the mailbox, or be buried under a frozen pizza. When my keys are lost, I get frustrated because I have to spend valuable time searching for them again. Like most moms who multi-task in so many directions at once, my attempts to retrace my steps are darn near impossible. After I throw off my coat, I put the eggs in the refrigerator, preheat the oven, answer a few e-mails, devour a granola bar, walk the dog, wipe the sticky countertop, and separate darks and lights without paying much attention to where I put my keys. Not until I get back in the car again to take the kids to the orthodontist do I realize that my keys are even missing again. I would surrender to the extra set of keys if I could remember where I keep the emergency spares.

Funny how I lecture my kids on how to put their things away when they finish using them, whether it's math homework, sweaty socks, or dirty dishes. So when I shout, "Where are my keys?!" for the hundredth time, they have every right to say, "Wherever you left them, mom."

Angels Among Us

The other night I was driving my van on Clayton Road in Town and Country and I hit a deer. I saw the huge gray buck cross the road, but it was too late to swerve out of the way. No other cars were around me. I put my foot on the brake and gripped the steering wheel as I slammed into the side of the animal that suddenly appeared in my headlights. I'll never forget the gruesome image of its massive body tearing into pieces in front of my windshield. I was okay and no one else was involved. I prayed that the deer hadn't suffered. Somehow I stayed calm as I continued to drive straight ahead, slowly and cautiously. When I finally pulled into my garage at home, I got out of the car and was shocked to see the smashed hood and bumper. A chunk of deer hair was still stuck under the Nissan emblem. It grossed me out, but I knew how much worse the serious situation could have been.

I felt like someone was looking out for me that night. I wanted to say a prayer in gratitude. When we escape danger or recover from illness, we say "*Baruch Atah Adonai Eloheinu Melech ha'olam, sheg' malani kol tov.*" It means, "Thank You, God, for Your comfort in time of fear and Your kindness in my time of need."

Perhaps you've experienced the feeling that someone is watching over you, like a guardian angel. Some people believe that a protective spirit whispers to them through their gut instinct, hunch, or intuition. The word intuition, by the way, means "in to you" in Latin.

I try to pay attention to my inner voice, even if I sometimes ignore the message. I used to call this my Divine Spirit talking to me. Then again, I sat cross-legged on top of a vortex in Sedona and chanted "Oooommmm" in my earlier metaphysical days. Seriously, I believe that we're all born with a sixth sense or ESP that allows us to communicate beyond the physical realm.

Even the famous analytical psychologist Carl Jung said, "Until you make the unconscious conscious, it will direct your life and you will call it fate." The Swiss influential thinker wasn't Jewish, but his widely respected philosophies are reflected in the roots of Judaism.

Sure enough, the sources of the angels used in kabbalah and ceremonial magic are primarily Jewish. The word angel is derived from the Christian Latin *angelos*, itself derived from the Greek *aggelos*, which is a translation of the Hebrew word *mal ach*, a messenger.

The Hebrew word for letter, *ot*, also means sign or wonder or miracle. For thousands of years, Jewish sages have taught that the letters of the Hebrew Alphabet, the *Aleph Beit*, embody wonderfully miraculous powers.

No wonder the idea of something unexplainable like an angel makes sense to me.

God Bless Chocolate

The other day I'm sitting in the vet's office waiting for Luci to get her vaccines and I start to feel antsy and bored. A talking parrot next to me is imitating the meows of a sick cat and I'm about to lose my mind. Even Luci paces the room like a prisoner in a jail cell.

It's times like this when I'm desperate to pass the time in a productive way. The only thing I can think of is to clean out my messy purse. It makes me feel like I've really accomplished something every time I throw away chewing gum wrappers, crossed-out shopping lists, broken toothpicks, and whatever else I find crushed and crumbled in the bottom of my bag. The other day I actually salvaged a Chuck E. Cheese token, which is odd because I haven't been there since 1999.

On this particular afternoon, however, I discover gold—or the next best thing—chocolate!—buried underneath my car keys and coupons. I hurriedly dig out the single piece of Dove chocolate and as I pop the sweet and creamy morsel in my mouth all my problems suddenly melt away. Sure I feel a little guilty as I hand Luci a stale milk bone, but I deserve a treat, too.

Surprisingly, my "mmmm" turns into a "hmmmm" when I notice the message inside the red foil wrapper. It reads, "The wind tells a story. Listen."

When our appointment is finally over, my poodle and I walk to the car and those words stick with me. I try to block out Luci barking at the other dogs and pay closer attention to the sounds of nature. Finally, a gust of wind blows my way, or maybe it's exhaust fumes from a dump truck next to me, and my ears perk up. I hear something tell me to drive to the nearest Walgreens and buy a bag of Dove Promises Mini Chocolates.

I look at all the flavors: milk chocolate, dark chocolate, peanut butter, chocolate almond, chocolate bananas foster, chocolate caramel, dark chocolate tiramisu, and even a special Susan

G. Komen pack that gives hopeful messages to breast cancer survivors, such as: "Early detection saves lives" and "Do a little something special for yourself everyday" and "Always remember you are beautiful."

I can't decide, so I buy a bag of each and a bottle of Pepto-Bismol. I justify my binge as research. I already feel my blood sugar rising.

I waste no time unwrapping the candy and I'm tickled by sayings like "It's definitely a bubble-bath day" and "Sometimes a smile can mean more than a dozen roses" and "Chocolate is my only vice," which I save inside my wallet. Even though I'm no longer hungry, I crave more words of wisdom, such as "If at first you don't succeed then skydiving isn't for you" and "Keep your friends close and your chocolate closer."

Now I feel sick, but I'm addicted to the pep talk, not to mention the intoxicating pure cocoa butter. It goes on, "Believe in your dreams" and "Be the first to hit the dance floor" and "Call your mom" and "Carve out a little moment for yourself."

It turns out that I can visit the Dove chocolate website, www. dovechocolate.com, and submit my own messages of inspiration, romance, life, friendship, hope, whatever. Here's a perfect opportunity to spread the love in a way only Jewish people can. Although I didn't come up with these sayings, here are some of my favorites:

"Where there's smoke, there may be salmon."
"No meal is complete without leftovers."
"One *mitzvah* can change the world; two will just make you tired."
"Anything worth saying is worth repeating a thousand times."
"Never take a front row seat at a *bris*."
"Next year in Jerusalem. The year after that, how about a nice

cruise?"
"Never leave a restaurant empty handed."
"Spring ahead, fall back, winter in Florida."
"Without Jewish mothers, who would need therapy?"
"If you have to ask the price, you can't afford it. But if you can afford it, make sure to tell everybody what you paid."
"Don't give up. Moses was once a basket case."
"What part of 'Thou shalt not' don't you understand?"

Finally, "What is the most common disease transmitted by Jewish mothers? Guilt."

Bottom line, always save room for chocolate.

Bieber Fever Is Contagious

Go ahead and make fun of me. I can take it. I'm a big girl. I openly admit that I'm a fan of 16-year-old singing sensation Justin Bieber—you know, the cute kid with the signature hairdo, perfect skin, and the guts to dance on stage alongside his mentor Usher like no other white boy I've ever seen.

Even though I don't have the pop star's poster on my bedroom wall, I still felt like a giddy "Belieber" when I took Sari and a bunch of her girlfriends to the opening night of the wildly anticipated movie *Never Say Never*.

Sure I felt a little out of place as I chewed sugarless gum and waited in line with hysterical middle schoolers who tied purple bandanas around their heads, texted each other on their bling-encrusted cell phones (even though they were standing right next to each other), and munched on popcorn despite wearing neon-colored braces that cost their parents a fortune.

The theatre was packed with screaming pubescent girls who

pretended that the 3D movie was a real live rock concert. They actually stood on their feet and stretched out their arms waiting for their dimply idol to throw his sweaty baseball cap into the audience. I took another mom with me and we looked like dorks wearing black-framed plastic eyeglasses as we sat behind our daughters. As you probably already know, never sit in the same row with your kids. It cramps their style and it's just not cool.

The movie was a lot of fun and not one time did Bieber grab his crotch. Not only that, his songs contained absolutely no cuss words or pornographic lyrics, unlike Grammy winner Rhianna whose song about S&M blares on every radio station these days. Instead, Bieber wows his multigenerational audience with his genuine musical talent, unstoppable energy, adorable smile, and, even though it's not my thing, underwear hanging out of his baggy pants.

This biographical documentary traces Bieber's incredible rise to fame from the time he was a toddler and banged on his drum set, strummed his guitar, and belted out tunes for his close-knit family and friends. The movie also shows that he is, in many ways, a normal kid who likes to eat McDonald's chicken nuggets, ride his motor scooter, shoot hoops with his buddies, squirt water guns at his crew, say grace before his meals, and sell out Madison Square Garden in 22 minutes. Okay, so he's not a typical teenager.

I'm not prejudiced that Bieber was discovered on YouTube by a Jewish guy named Scott Samuel "Scooter" Braun, who taught Bieber, a Christian, how to pray the *Shema* before a concert. I just think the cute boy with the hair is an inspiration to young people, and his message is believe in yourself, work hard, and follow your dreams.

I couldn't have said it better myself.

Jewish Moms Win Big At The Oscars

I'm obsessed with celebrities. I know it's wrong, but I usually park my shopping cart in the longest line at the grocery store so that I can take my time and flip through *People* magazine.

So it's no surprise that the Academy Awards ceremony is a much-anticipated television event at my house, ranking right up there with *American Idol* and the Super Bowl. Oscars 2011 was particularly exciting because Jewish moms were in the spotlight.

Setting the precedent was James Franco, the adorable co-host and best-actor nominee for *127 Hours,* who introduced his mother and grandmother in the audience. I can't imagine what brings a mother more *naches*—to witness her son dress as Marilyn Monroe on stage at the Kodak Theatre in front of millions of viewers or the fact that he's earning his Ph.D. in English at Yale University.

The *kvelling* continued when Tom Hooper accepted the top prize as best director for *The Kings Speech.* His mom beamed when her son credited her for giving him the idea to do this film in the first place. It just goes to show you, he said in his speech, "Always listen to your mother."

The next proud moment came when mommy-to-be Natalie Portman took the stage and accepted her best-actress award for her brilliantly disturbing portrayal of a tortured ballerina in *Black Swan.* The Israeli-born Jew was glowing in purple silk chiffon and, just as she did in her speeches at the Golden Globes and Screen Actors Guild, she acknowledged her parents for all their love and support. The teary eyed actress also thanked her boyfriend, choreographer Benjamin Millepied, her film dance partner, for giving her the greatest role of her life: motherhood.

Chapter 7
Dog Is God Spelled Backwards

We Love Luci

Every mother should own a dog, even if her child is allergic
to furry animals and has to sleep in a tent in the backyard. If
a mother's love has no boundaries, then her need to nurture
extends to the four-legged kind as well. My toy poodle Luci is
an integral part of my family—more so than some of my blood
relatives—and she poses for all of our holiday cards. Weighing
less than a gallon of milk, my fluffy apricot pup provides the kind
of comfort, companionship, and unconditional love that no one
else comes close to. I can't remember the last time my husband
licked my face or my kids brought me the newspaper without
expecting an allowance in return.

I didn't always feel this way. I never had a dog growing up,
just two hamsters, a crawdad, and a goldfish. So when my kids
begged me for a dog, I tried to convince them otherwise and
bribed them with an iguana. I even wrote an article for "Pet

Gazette" magazine on why I didn't want a dog, including the fact that my husband suffered from animal-induced asthma. Plus, my kids are finally potty trained and sleep through the night—why would I want to start over with a puppy at this point in my life?

Luci, 6 weeks old, weighs less than 2 pounds, September 2003.

Then everything changed one fateful summer day three years ago when the *St. Louis Post-Dispatch* Sunday edition landed on our driveway, and we don't even subscribe to it. I remember the strange sight of Scott sitting at the kitchen table in his flannel boxers with his head buried in a cereal bowl and the classifieds. I assumed he was circling ads for Toyotas, not toy poodles. After breakfast, I knew I was in trouble when he walked out the door with a grin on his face and the newspaper rolled under his arm. His last words to me were, "Don't worry, honey. I'm just going to look at the new puppies. I won't buy any."

Needless to say, when Scott showed up later that day at a friend's pool party with a bloated hamster-looking pup in the palm of his hand, my heart melted into my margarita. Like any proud papa he announced, "It's a girl!" Everyone rushed to see the six-week-old puppy with a little pink tongue and stub of a tail. We wasted no time giving the funny little redhead her name when everyone agreed, "We Love Luci!"

A Mom's Best Friend

Anyone who knows me knows that I'm crazy about my dog, or maybe they just think I'm crazy. When Luci was the size of a Beanie Baby, I carried her around town before Paris Hilton made it hip to tote a teeny pooch inside a Coach purse. Luci and I dined together at Cardwell's at Plaza Frontenac, shopped for back-to-school snacks at Sam's Club, and picked up the kids in carpool line every day. Maybe I love her so much because she satisfies my baby fix without the hassles of diapers, pacifiers, and colic. To be honest, I would rather carry a pooper-scooper than a bottle.

Unlike my children, my dog never will grow up. Luci loves to nap anywhere and anytime. My kids would rather torture me than go to sleep. Luci lets me hold her like a favorite stuffed teddy bear and smooch her face whenever I want. My kids are embarrassed when I kiss their forehead in the school parking lot.

Luci is always in a good mood and ready to play. My kids ride a daily emotional roller coaster, being best friends and worst enemies in the time it takes me to make a peanut butter sandwich. When I baby talk to Luci, she looks me in the eye and cocks her head like she understands. My kids speak a language all their own and tune me out after only a few sentences.

Luci still bathes in the kitchen sink. I'm lucky if my kids wash their hands without me nagging them. Luci follows me around wherever I go and sits patiently next to me when I write at the computer. My kids seem to disappear whenever I need their help with anything.

I rarely discipline Luci because she usually learns from her mistakes, like that time she chewed an electric cord and literally flew across the room in shock. When my kids fight with each other, I send them to their rooms for punishment, but it never seems to make a difference for very long.

Luci snuggles in bed with me every night and has her own pillow. If my daughter comes into my room in the middle of the night, she lies on the floor. After a stressful day, when Luci jumps into my lap and curls up, she is as warm and soft as a cashmere blanket. In moments like this, my dog pampers me like a long soak in a hot tub, a one-pound Hershey's bar with almonds, and a glass of Chardonnay all rolled into one furry little animal. Nothing is more relaxing, except maybe a day spa.

Luci and Me, November 2009.

And like that's going to happen.

Everything I Need To Know I Learned From My Dog

Sometimes the most important lessons in life come from unexpected teachers, such as my dog. Here's what my six-pound poodle has taught me:

- Always wake up in a good mood.
- Love unconditionally—it's your number one priority.
- Don't hold grudges. Forgive easily.
- If you're dirty, clean yourself.
- Don't judge people by how they look. Treat everyone equally.
- Give lots of kisses.
- Be loyal.

- Protect your loved ones and your property.
- Chase butterflies.
- Play hard.
- Watch leaves flutter to the ground. Stay curious about everything.
- When you're tired, take a break. Better yet, sneak in a nap.
- Enjoy the cool breeze and warm sun on your face.
- When you're thirsty, drink lots of clean water.
- Get plenty of rest and exercise.
- Comfort people when they're sick or sad. Kiss away tears.
- Be there.
- Cuddle often.
- Bark, but don't bite.
- Lay in the grass.
- Play in the snow.
- Never pass up an opportunity to go for a walk or play ball.
- Smell something before you eat it.
- Learn how to relax.
- Sit up straight.
- Follow your instinct.
- Be cautious of strangers.
- When you have an itch, scratch it.
- Stretch your arms and legs. Stay limber. Curl your body into a ball sometimes.
- When someone in your family comes home from work or school, greet him or her like you haven't seen each other in years.
- Run circles around the big guys.
- Being small makes you mighty, strong, nimble, and fast.
- Make friends easily.
- Be brave when you hear a strange noise in the middle of the night.

- When you're feeling cute, flaunt it.
- Look people in the eye when they talk to you.
- When you're excited about something, don't hold back.
- Pay attention to body language. If someone's tail and head are down, give them space.
- When your belly is full, leave food in your bowl.
- Then again, there's always room for dessert.
- Don't eat garbage; it'll make you sick.
- Never give up. Keep digging for what you want.
- It's the journey, not the destination, so enjoy the ride with the windows down.

Bless The Pets

I can't imagine life without Luci. She is my baby, my third child who'll never grow up. She'll never tire of my kisses and cuddling. She's my profile picture on my Facebook page, for God's sake.

As all of us pet owners already know, animals are a gift from God. Remember, the word dog is God spelled backwards. So when I had the opportunity to bless Luci at a recent animal prayer ceremony at our temple, I had to be there. After all, my little furry, four-legged companion deserves a special prayer that shows my gratitude for her boundless love and loyalty, even if she causes me aggravation when she runs across the street to eat cookie crumbs in my neighbor's backyard.

So a group of us gathered on a chilly autumn morning in the parking lot while our best friends wagged their tails and sniffed each other. Instead of *yarmulkes*, the dogs donned blue scarves tied around their necks. The temple has hosted the annual blessing of the pets for several years, but this was the first time that all of the guests of honor were dogs. All of God's creatures, by the way, are welcome, and in the past people have brought their cats, hermit crabs, and even a stuffed teddy bear. The rabbi leads us in prayer.

We say together: "May God who blessed our ancestors, Abraham, Isaac, and Jacob, Sarah, Rebecca, Rachel, and Leah, bless all the animals who are part of our lives—the dogs, cats, birds, fish, reptiles, and all other pets who live with us in our homes, who take care of us as much as we take care of them, who teach us the values of caring and compassion, and who bring joy into our homes through their unique personalities, who seem to have the uncanny ability to sit by us when we are sick and to jump up and down when we are well and ready to play, who never ask for much other than to be fed and whose constant companionship and friendship to us is as strong and real as ours is to them. Thank you, God, for the wonders of your creation, which includes such wonderful animals who are part of our lives, and for directing these special creatures to our homes and to our care."

On this Saturday morning, surrounded by colorful falling leaves, our diverse group includes rescue dogs, therapy dogs, lap dogs, and more. There's Cody, a mix of Bichon Frise and Cavalier King Charles Spaniel; Zach, a Morkie, or a mix of a Maltese and Yorkie; Tucker, an English Springer Spaniel; Daisy, a Cockapoo; Bailey, a Golden Retriever; Wiggins, a Soft Coated Wheaten Terrier; Teddi, a Bichon Frise, whose pure white coat is as puffy as a cloud against the bright blue sky; and Henry, a Pug rescued from a puppy mill.

Pet blessings occur throughout the year but escalate in October during the celebrations of the Catholic Feast Day of Saint Francis of Assisi, the patron saint of animals, and World Animal Day. The origin of the Jewish ritual is not as obvious, but nonetheless has been sacred for centuries because the Jews have always valued animals. The story of Noah's Ark says it all.

Has Dieting Gone To The Dogs?

We all know that obesity is a huge problem—more than two-thirds of adults in the United States are overweight—but now we've gone too far. According to a recent article in *The Wall Street Journal*, even our pets have gotten pouchy in their *pipeks*. In fact, the Association for Pet Obesity Prevention, which conducted a survey with Mars Inc.'s Banfield Pet Hospital, the nation's largest general veterinary practice, reports that more than half of U.S. dogs and cats are considered overweight or obese, which is defined as 30 percent above normal weight.

What's next—our furry four-legged friends suffer from anxiety and swallow a little Prozac pill hidden inside a glob of peanut butter? Sadly enough, mental illness actually does affect some of the animals we love. Now man's best friend is fat *and* depressed.

For thousands of years, Judaism has emphasized kindness to animals. Under Jewish law, in fact, we are obligated to take good care of the health of our pets. For example, we are required to feed our household pets before ourselves and allow them to rest on Shabbat. We are also forbidden to muzzle an ox to prevent it from eating while working in the field, according to Deuteronomy, but that's another story.

Let's face it. In many cases, dogs are plump because their owners are lazy. To them, I say, "Get off your butt and walk your canine companion around the block a few times! It wouldn't hurt you."

In addition to not exercising enough, overfeeding dogs is a big no-no. And serving them table scraps doesn't help matters. I admit that I sometimes give Luci people food. Then again, she also sits at the dinner table with us. Well, she is part of the family. But Luci keeps her girlish figure with plenty of running up and down the steps, jumping on and off the bed, and chasing squirrels outside.

Seriously, excess weight on cats and dogs can cause severe and costly health problems, including diabetes, arthritis, kidney failure, high blood pressure, and cancer. In fact, obesity is the single most preventable health crisis facing the country's 171 million-plus dog and cat pets. Diet plans and doggy treadmills are ways to trim the waistline, but nothing beats going for a walk, breathing in fresh air, and sniffing the behind of a canine companion, for a dog, that is.

Chapter 8
Holy Matrimony!

Space Brings Us Closer Together

Parenting experts profess that the secret to raising happy, well-adjusted kids is for married couples to make their relationship a priority. (Single parents have their own challenges.) The traditional Jewish ideal of *shelom bayit* backs up the idea that a marriage based on mutual love and respect is the foundation for creating a spiritually enriching home for your children.

In other words, hire a babysitter or bribe the grandparents to give you and your spouse a break from the young ones now and then. Whether you catch a movie, peddle your bikes in the park, or recover the lost art of conversation, spouses need to reconnect with each other in order to be better parents.

In all honesty, I admire couples that actually stick to their commitment to spend time together, even when their children's itineraries drag them in opposite directions. And until I figure out how to actually do that, I suggest another way for moms to maintain marital bliss, only my idea doesn't involve my husband or my kids.

First, I pack a suitcase. Next, I kiss everyone goodbye. Finally, I get out of town, even if only for a few days. That's right—I leave Jack and Sari with their dad to bond while I relax and rejuvenate somewhere, anywhere. I rationalize that my husband gets to go to work everyday, so my little getaway is only fair. Maybe, just maybe, when I do return home, my family might better understand what I accomplish in an average day, including laundry, meal preparation, play date coordination, endless errands, fist fight patrol, chauffeur, and dog vomit cleanup. Even if they still don't appreciate what I do as a mom, who cares. At least I got away, right?

I was lucky enough to really get out of Dodge last year when I went horseback riding in Colorado with a handful of adventurous moms. We called ourselves Wild Women of the West. I climbed 10,000 feet up the Rocky Mountains on a horse named Itchy. There was no doubt that I was far from home when our cocky trail guide, a rugged, leather-faced cowboy, introduced himself in a slow, western drawl. "I'm Stu, and that ain't short for stupid." His bushy mustache was stained from a lifetime of harsh sunlight and cigarettes.

In the rear of the line was our long-time friend Doug MacGregor, a retired businessman turned cowboy, who lives in Denver and coordinated every muddy clop of this unforgettable adventure. Not even the light drizzle dampened our spirits on this journey, and we never stopped laughing for long. In fact, I found it amusing when rain collected in the ridges of my brand new straw cowboy hat. Every time I leaned forward in my saddle, water fell into my lap. Never mind that I was forced to wear an oversized, torn, yellow slicker that covered my cool western attire, including a blue bandana tied in a knot around my neck. I took in the splendor of the snow-capped mountains and rows of dark green pine trees that went on forever.

At the end of the two-and-a-half-hour ride, I ungripped the reins and slid off my horse. That's when I realized that I could barely walk to the car because I pulled a muscle somewhere along the way. Despite my severely stiff knees, I savored every moment, including a herd of elk roaming alongside the highway. I dined on the best gazpacho and deviled eggs that I've ever tasted. Thanks to the hospitality of Doug and his wife Claire, who opened their home and their hearts to us, I never once felt guilty about leaving my clan behind on this trip. Well, maybe for a second, but I got over it after my second glass of Chardonnay.

I knew deep in my heart that I deserved this time to myself. Everyone benefits when mom feels energized again. Besides, Scott and the kids enjoyed their own adventure while I was away. For starters, they built several forts, including a hut made of willow branches that still stands in the backyard. Every time I look at the tree limbs and wood scraps tied together with rope in the shape of a teepee, I remember my special mountain experience. And I realize that I don't have to travel very far to live an adventure.

Gift-Giving Guide For Husbands

If it's a *mitzvah* for a Jew to marry, then it's an even greater deed for a wife to put up with her husband's annoying habits. One of my top 10 complaints about Scott is his inability to read my mind, especially when it comes to knowing what kind of gift makes me happy. After 13 years of marriage, the only person I can change is myself, right? So from now on, I am going to either hand Scott a detailed list of what I want or I will go to Victoria's Secret and buy the satin pajamas myself. That way, there's no surprises, no disappointments, and no hurt feelings.

Of course, I would love for my better half to bestow me with unexpected tokens of his affection, such as a handful of tropical orchids or a chunk of dark chocolate almond bark. Even though surprises like this make me feel special, I try to be realistic about a guy who wants to boycott Valentine's Day because the roses shrivel up and die anyway.

No matter what the occasion, I tell him that fresh flowers are always an option, even if the purple irises are grown in my own backyard and arranged in a vase. Plus, my mother taught me a long time ago that the presentation is as important as the present. Over the years, her gifts usually come wrapped in polka dots, stripes, or some kind of fancy paper and are topped with a curly ribbon and Hallmark card. To this day, she still creases the corners and tapes the package so tight that I feel guilty as I rip it open. Then again, I get the same pleasure when I unravel anything that my kids cover in white tissue paper and a roll of Scotch tape.

Scott, on the other hand, doesn't understand why I fuss over the frill. His idea of going all out is a Chico's shopping bag. This year's birthday gift, however, was the icing on the cake. (What cake, by the way?) He wrapped my present in a red fleece blanket from the car that we use to sit on the ground at sporting events. To give you a better idea of my predicament, I'll let you eavesdrop on part of our conversation that went downhill from here:

Scott: "Do you want your birthday present a day early?"
Me: "That depends. Did you get a chance to wrap it first?"
Scott: "I hid the box in the trunk of my car so you wouldn't find it."
Me: "Okay, well, then I wonder what it is?"
Scott: "Ta da! Happy birthday babe! Hope you like it!"

Me: "My gosh, the box is so heavy. Why is it wrapped in a blanket with a dried leaf stuck on top?"

Scott: "I didn't have time to wrap it."

Me: "Whatever. The outside of the box shows a hot water dispenser. What's inside?"

Scott: "I thought because you love to drink hot tea so much, a hot water dispenser will save you time and make it easier because you don't have to use the microwave or wait for the water to boil. Isn't that cool?"

Me: "Well, actually it's really hot. I hope the kids don't burn their hands when they mistake it for the kitchen faucet."

Scott: "Don't worry. You can use the hot water dispenser to also make hot chocolate, oatmeal, and even JELL-O!"

Me: "I don't know whether to laugh or cry."

Scott: "What's the matter? You don't like it? I'll take it back if you're not going to use it."

Me: "No, we can keep it. I guess I can always use another kitchen appliance."

Scott: "If you don't like it, you can return it to Home Depot and pick out something else you like."

Me: "Gee honey, thanks a lot."

Scott: "You never like anything I get you."

Me: "That's not true. What about the gift certificate for the body massage and facial that I picked up at the beauty salon myself and let you pay for? I really like that."

Scott: "A spa package is boring, and I already gave one to you. The hot water dispenser, on the other hand, is something different and practical because you can enjoy it over and over again."

Me: "I understand what you're saying, but a hot water dispenser is not birthday material. It would have been more appropriate to give it to me a week before or after my birthday as a 'just-because' gift, and then maybe I would appreciate it more."

Scott: "I can't do anything right."

The truth is, Scott does a lot of things right, like when he steam cleans the carpet or takes the kids to soccer practice if I have another candle party to attend on our block. Besides, I try to convince him that I'm not a high-maintenance wife who needs diamond earrings to make me happy. He knows that I'm a sucker for sentiment, and I go nuts over those stepping stones decorated with the kids' handprints. Even a travel mug filled with yummy Chai tea mix warms my heart, as does a picnic basket filled with munchies and a note that says we'll dine alfresco today.

Oh well, there's always our anniversary.

Love Is In The Air. So Are Mold Spores

Even though Valentine's Day is named after two Christian martyrs named Valentine—that's at least one of the theories—a Jewish woman nevertheless worships this romantic holiday. She loves to be loved, and Hallmark makes it official. It doesn't seem to matter that the price of long stem roses quadruples in mid-February. Flowers are symbolic of love and romance, so there. Deep inside, she desires to be treated like the unsuspecting actress in the Zales commercials.

A mom with young children especially likes the element of surprise—not the kind she uncovers in a dirty diaper, but the one she discovers when she gently opens a small velvet box. She also likes attention—not the kind she gets from a toddler's temper tantrum in a shopping mall, but when her husband notices her new hairdo before he finds the beauty salon receipt. She likes to feel special. So what else is new?

Valentine's Day has been around a long time. The holiday of hearts originated when courtly love flourished in the high Middle Ages. Centuries later, this cold, winter holiday is hotter than ever. In fact, the Greeting Card Association estimates one billion valentines are sent each year worldwide, and this doesn't include the boxes of cards moms buy for their children's school parties. Obviously, women are more sentimental because we purchase 85 percent of all valentine cards.

Valentine's Day is the traditional day for couples to express their feelings of love for each other, even if they fight over the MasterCard bill earlier that same morning. At some point before the alarm clock is reset, wives and husbands across America are expected to kiss and make up, which for me usually involves chocolate. I'm easy.

In Jewish tradition, a special day for sweethearts falls on the fifteenth day of the month of *Av*, which is usually late August. This festival of love is called *Tu B'Av*. In ancient times, girls in white dresses danced in the vineyards, where the boys awaited them. In modern Israeli culture, *Tu B'Av* is a popular day to pronounce love, propose marriage, and give tokens of affections like cards or flowers.

But who wants to wait until the summer to officially declare their devotion? Jewish wisdom tells us to take advantage of any opportunity to celebrate our relationships, whether it's with our significant other, children, or family. When it comes to marriage, the sages remind us that no love is perfect, and this important lifelong lesson is loud and clear from the time the groom shatters a glass under his foot. From the wedding day forward, Judaism emphasizes that our struggles and efforts to make our relationships better and stronger are what counts.

So, with that in mind, here are a few simple and inexpensive ways for wives to make their husbands feel special on Valentine's Day:

1. For a toasty treat, surprise your spouse and throw his socks in

the dryer before he gets dressed. (Note: Your husband should not be wearing those socks at the time the pair is tumbling in the Maytag.)

2. Buy him your favorite chocolate and hope he'll share.

3. Make dinner reservations so that he won't have to.

4. Slip a note in his briefcase that says something affectionate like, "Be home early."

5. Let him be in charge of the remote control for one night.

6. Finally, don't criticize him for 24 hours. I know, that's a tough one, but it's only for a day.

It Takes Two To Tango

I'm always looking for a new adventure, so I recently signed Scott and me up for ballroom dance classes. Sounds corny, but ballroom dancing has never been hotter, thanks to the hit show *Dancing With The Stars*. But the Olympic speed skater and dancing champion Apollo Anton Ohno is not my inspiration for taking a group dance class. I just want to spend some quality time with my hubby, get a little exercise, have fun, and learn how to swing my partner without making fools of ourselves. Bottom line, I want to feel light on my feet without counting calories.

So, one hour a week, we agree to trip the light fantastic and try not to trip each other. It's time to polish some of our rusty dance moves that until now consist of the bump from the original disco era. Even at my own wedding reception, I stumbled during the electric slide and blamed my clumsiness on too much champagne.

Over the years, slow dancing can get a little dull when you don't know what you're doing. Basically, many married couples hold hands and sway with an instrumental version of "Ribbon in the Sky" in the background. Sometimes, Scott and I manage to talk about practical things like the grocery list or the next day's dentist appointments while we hold each other close. This closeness is nice, but we have the potential to do so much more on the slippery parquet dance floor.

Needless to say, I'm ready to spice up our dance repertoire and try something hot like salsa dancing. I want to taste some fancy footwork that makes Latin ballroom dance so exciting to watch. Come on, if Jerry Springer can learn how to waltz and strut his stuff on television, anything's possible. I look forward to learning the foxtrot, samba, cha-cha, and all the other dances that make everything old seem new again. Too bad we miss the first four classes because of a baseball game, a Jewish holiday, a teacher conference, and the fact that I forgot to schedule this activity in my day planner.

When we finally make it to our first session at the nearby studio, I feel out of place right away. First of all, we are late because Scott never gets home from work on time and if he does, then he barely swallows his macaroni and cheese before we have to dash out the door again. Our instructor is a professional dancer named Amanda, who is the size of Tinker Bell and looks half my age. She always has a big smile and makes us feel welcome despite our tardiness.

We partner up right away. Not surprisingly, the ladies outnumber the men, so the female students have to dance with each other when we rotate partners. Amanda reminds us to stand up straight, keep our arms strong, lift our chest, and squeeze our abs. The perfect posture feels so unnatural when I slump most of the day. To make matters worse, the mirrored walls don't lie either. Everywhere I turn I see my clumsy reflection laughing at me. I can't help but feel self-conscious. While the other students practice their poise and gracefully twirl, I worry what I look like. In fact, I shock myself when I notice that I left the house without brushing my hair and changing my ketchup-stained shirt. I also realize that I'm the only one wearing flip-flops, while everyone else has on closed-toe shoes. I quickly learn my lesson when Scott smashes my toes.

One of my favorite numbers is the merengue because the directions are basically eight steps to the right, eight steps to the left, eight steps in a circle, and repeat. We shake our hips, stroke each other's arms, and start to feel the music. It gets kind of steamy during this Latin favorite, if you know what I mean. Then again, the air conditioner is broken. When Scott and I gaze into each other's eyes, I feel like we're on a romantic date. In my ear, he whispers, "You have lettuce in your teeth."

So much for romance. At least we know the hora.

Shedding Pounds Weighs Heavy On My To-Do List

Every night before I fall asleep clutching my body pillow, I make the next day's to-do list in my head. I don't recommend this bedtime ritual for insomniacs, by the way. My random thoughts might include: go to the bank/grocery store; drop Luci off at the groomer; write a story that makes half sense; meet girlfriends for lunch; attend variety show rehearsal; find Jack a ride to basketball practice; take Sari to Hebrew school; help with school science fair; make doctor's appointment; clean the basement; buy new indoor soccer shoes; revise menu with caterer; save the environment; and, oh yeah, lose weight for the upcoming *bar mitzvah*.

As Scott aims the remote at the television and switches back and forth between the news and *Everybody Loves Raymond*, my mental notes seem overwhelming. I worry that I might forget to do something on my list. The internal banter continues:

Me: "Did I leave any candles burning downstairs?"

Me: "I haven't changed the batteries in the smoke detectors in a long time."

Me: "Is the garage door closed?"

Me: "I hope nobody breaks into the house in the middle of the night."

Me: "Did I leave behind a kid who I was supposed to pick up at the batting cages?"

Me: "No one ever will ask me to carpool again. I'm an irresponsible, horrible mom."

Me: "I just spent $200 at the grocery store and what am I making for dinner?"

Me: "I'll try to use my expired coupons for Pasta House."

Me: "How am I going to drop two dress sizes in two months?"

Me: "Good luck."

There I am, lost in my thoughts again, when I finally blurt out, "Scott, we've got to get in shape for the *bar mitzvah*, honey, and I mean it. Starting tomorrow, it's time to stop eating and start moving."

"You're right," he agrees, half-asleep. "Right after I finish the leftover chocolate cake for breakfast."

There's nothing like a big event, whether it's my child's *bar mitzvah*, a family wedding, a college reunion, or a beach vacation, that motivates me to lose a few pounds and try to feel my best. It also helps when Scott and I work together as a team and encourage each other to live healthier. If time spent working on a computer counts as physical exercise, Scott and I both would qualify as triathletes. I also like my version of the Stairmaster, in which I work up a sweat carrying loads of laundry up and down the stairs. To increase my heart rate, I sprint in my bare feet to the mailbox when the wind chill is below zero.

Scott and I are serious about trimming down for Jack's *bar mitzvah.* We realize that the first thing we need to do is change our eating habits and lifestyle. Instead of snacking on ice cream, for example, we plan to nibble on celery sticks. Another goal is to wake up early on the weekends and power walk around the neighborhood, no matter how cold or tired we are. We even decided to cut the carbs, except challah on the Sabbath meal, of course. We have God's blessing.

Even though we don't like the idea of going on diets (remember that the first three letters in diet are die), we want to familiarize ourselves with the most popular weight-loss plans. Here are a few, not in any particular order:

1. Atkins (no bagels, no sugar, no way).
2. The Zone (no caffeine, no diet soda, no chance).
3. Grapefruit Diet (counteracts with cholesterol medicine).
4. Weight Watchers (embarrassed to get weighed in front of people).
5. Macrobiotic Diet (no meat, no yogurt, and what's twig tea?).
6. Detox Diets (I gave up on my metabolism years ago).
7. The GI Diet (has nothing to do with soldiers but something called the glycemic index).
8. Rosemary Conley's Hip and Thigh Diet (sounds too much like the late, great, and overweight Rosemary Clooney. Besides, hips are not our problem. What about *pipeks*?).

Let's face it. Losing weight is a losing battle. Hopefully, with lots of willpower, we can win this one together.

Chapter 9
The *Bar/Bat Mitzvah* Sagas

Planning Dream *Bar Mitzvah* Is A Nightmare

Let the countdown begin. It's officially time to freak out about my son's *bar mitzvah*, which is scheduled in March 2008. I know what you're thinking. It's a year away. What took me so long? What can I say, except that I've never planned this kind of lifecycle event, not even a *bris*, which only my obstetrician was invited to.

So far, this is what I have in mind, roughly. First and foremost, I either book the synagogue or a plane ticket to Israel. Next, I find a place for the reception and make a down payment on an eight-piece rock band that includes motivational dancers, a laser light show, live video cams, and a full-blown sound system that causes everyone to need hearing aids. Then, I secure a videographer, photographer, caterer, florist, and whoever else convinces me that I need their services. Right away, I hire a party planner to add her two cents when it comes to a theme, decorations, invitations, calligrapher, menu, centerpieces, place cards, seating chart, slide show, more entertainment, party favors, and the name of a reputable therapist for me to visit when this is all through.

Quick, I find a hotel and request a block of rooms for out-of-town guests, including those who my pre-adolescent son has never met before. Meanwhile, I keep everything a secret so that no one steals what I think is an original idea. Eventually, I scramble to update mailing addresses from both sides of the family and then hassle my husband to input the data into a spreadsheet. Sooner than later, I get a "real" job to help pay for this *bar mitzvah* blowout. Finally, after all the contracts are signed and reservations are made, I ask Jack what kind of coming-of-age ceremony he would like.

"I want to become a *bar mitzvah* in the rabbi's office. And I don't want anyone else in the room," he tells me, matter-of-factly. "Afterwards, I want to eat pizza and play basketball with my friends. And one more thing, no girls."

So, while Jack continues to focus on his Hebrew studies and prepares for his *D'var Torah*, it looks like I have my work cut out for me, too. While I embark on a party planning and spiritual journey of my own, I have to remind myself what's really important in the year ahead. The term *bar mitzvah* means "obligated to perform the Jewish *mitzvot*," and this life-changing moment represents the beginning, not the finale, of the development of my son's Jewish identity. With that said, planning a *bar mitzvah* makes hosting a wedding seem like a piece of cake.

Modern *Bar Mitzvahs* Play The Name Game

The other day Jack had the nerve to ask, "Mom, did you buy my Hanukkah presents yet?" I stared at him in disbelief. Doesn't he realize that I just forked over $300 to get our dog's teeth cleaned? Or what about the check I wrote last month for his basketball registration? He must think that money grows on trees and those brand new black suede boots in my closet were free.

After I regained my composure, I mustered an answer for the clueless son of mine. "Your Hanukkah present this year is your upcoming *bar mitzvah*. And, by the way, your Jewish coming-of-age celebration also counts as your birthday, high school graduation, and wedding present as well."

Like most parents who are planning a *bar* or *bat mitzvah* for their teen, I can't help but feel overwhelmed with all the details and expenses, from the *kiddish* to the *kippots*. Of course, I want Jack's *bar mitzvah* to be a special day for him, one that he will always remember. In fact, one of the most popular ways to memorialize the sacred event is through monogramming everything in sight, from blue M&Ms to candy wrappers.

It's true. I'm caught up in the craziness to emboss my son's name on as many items as possible, although I draw the line at rolls of personalized toilet paper. Considering the first thing Jack's name appears on is the invitations, I had some tough decisions to make besides whether to go with lined envelopes or not. As we all know, stationery makes a statement and must reflect the theme (sports or casino), the tone (serious or fun), the season (winter or spring), and the budget (expensive or cheap). So I thought long and hard about the color of his Hebrew and English names. I could opt for black, blue, red, neon, rainbow, or shimmering copper to match his hair. Plus, I can pick an endless variety of fonts in formal, casual scripts, block style, funky, engraved, caps, lower case, or all of the above. Also, I can design his name horizontally, vertically, circular, backwards, or let the calligrapher decide.

Not only that, I can display Jack's name in bright lights like a Broadway star. Better yet, I can put his name on a grand entry banner that stretches across the auditorium, in case guests forget whose reception it is. Then, I can spell out J-A-C-K with either Mylar balloons or glittery Styrofoam cutouts or maybe both. Next, I can monogram his name on centerpieces, event programs, place cards, sign-in boards, candle lighting pieces, t-shirts, socks, napkins, picture frames, CD labels, fruit rollups (I swear), key rings, candy jars, backpacks, pens, baseball cards, Hershey's kisses, thank-you notes, and God only knows what else.

Now that I think about it, maybe I'll get Jack a personalized baseball leather *yarmulke* for Hanukkah. I can choose suede, satin, straw, silk, velvet, fabric, taffeta, or hand-knitted. Inside the skullcap I can print his name in silver, gold, brown, or black ink, or I can embroider his initials and add his picture for an extra fee. After all, it's only money. And the name says it all.

Baseball Theme Out In Left Field

Tell me if I've gone too far. And I want you to be brutally honest. I'm considering inviting Fredbird to Jack's *bar mitzvah*. I'm not talking about Uncle Fred "Fredbird" who lives in New Jersey and has a nose the shape of a hawk's beak. I mean Fredbird— everyone's favorite Cardinals mascot, who actually fits perfectly into the baseball theme of the *bar mitzvah* party.

At $150 for half an hour, the cartoonish redbird, which actually looks more like a giant chicken dressed in an oversized Cardinals jersey, is guaranteed to amuse all ages, give unlimited high-fives, and maybe sign autographs if we're lucky. Fredbird is not my idea, of course. I give all the credit to my friend Jamie, who is considered an experienced party planner after hosting her daughter's recent casino *bat mitzvah* bash. The other option is bribe her husband into wearing a rented bird costume in exchange for a full-course steak dinner at Stony River.

In addition to Fredbird, her other suggestions include asking a couple of peppy high school cheerleaders to catapult plush baseballs into the crowd, using a slingshot like they do at Busch Stadium. To set the mood, my entertainment consultant also recommends broadcasting one of America's most well-known and well-loved songs, *Take Me Out to the Ballgame*, at the *kiddish* luncheon.

I told her that I'd think about it.

Sure, I want the party to be fun. After chanting the *Sh'mini* in *Leviticus* everyday for six months, my son deserves a good time. Still, I have to ask myself, "What has happened to the sanctity of the most significant childhood birthday in the Jewish tradition?" In the Talmud the only accompanying ritual associated with the *bar mitzvah* is a blessing pronounced by the father thanking God for ending his responsibility for his son's observance of the *mitzvot*, "Blessed is He who has now freed me from the responsibility of this boy."

Nowhere in the historical Jewish text does it mention a DJ, ice sculpture, chocolate fountain, or Mylar balloons.

By the 14th century, sources provide the first reference to a public occasion marking a boy's coming of age. Still, no description of catered food stations, personalized t-shirts, or a deluxe photo album that contains as many pages at the Torah itself. By the 17th century, boys were expected to say the blessing and read Torah. They delivered talks, often on talmudic learning, called the *derashah*, at an afternoon *seudat mitzvah*. Again, nowhere do the rabbis discuss a country club sit-down dinner with a choreographed slide show, caricature artist, or roaming videographer.

For centuries, the *bar mitzvah* for boys (and more recently the *bat mitzvah* for girls) marks the beginning of participation in the prayer service and reciting

Jack poses next to his baseball *bar mitzvah* cutout, March 2008.
(photo by Don Siegel)

blessings over the Torah. For the most part, the ceremony itself has remained the same for generations, although contemporary *bar* and *bat mitzvahs* (*b'nei mitzvah* is the plural) sometimes incorporate the individual talents and interests of the student. Obviously, what has changed most over the last few decades, is how this *simcha* is celebrated. For many parents and their teens, the passage into adolescence means one big party that ranks right up there with a wedding.

Unfortunately, the emphasis on expensive, lavish events has the potential to shadow the purpose of the *b'nei mitzvah* experience, which is to empower our sons and daughters to explore their Jewish identities even deeper. At no other time in a child's life is a connection to Judaism more important than in these early teen years. As they grow up in a challenging society and face tough decisions, their Jewish culture and religion can be a valuable resource. The key is to hang on to their accomplishment and make a lifelong commitment to being Jewish at home, in the community, and in the world.

Crying Through My Speech

I'm working on my speech for Jack's *bar mitzvah*, and it's harder to write than I thought. I mean, how can I adequately put down into words my uttermost feelings of pride and joy for my first born, who has now reached a new status within Judaism? It seems like only yesterday when my son was eating soggy Cheerios with his fingers. Wait a minute…that was yesterday.

Since the best place to start a *bar mitzvah* speech is at the beginning, I might as well talk about the first time I laid eyes on Jack. He was an embryo. I vividly recall the dialogue between the nurse and myself during my first ultrasound at the doctor's office.

Nurse: "There's your peanut!"
Me: "You mean it's a boy?" I shouted and nearly jumped off the table.
Nurse: "I said 'peanut,' not 'penis.' Besides, it's too early to tell if the baby is a boy or girl." She shook her head and rolled her eyes at me like I was another hyper new mom.
Me: "Oh, that's good, because I wanted the sex of the baby to be a surprise," I laughed in embarrassment as I grabbed the black and white ultrasound picture and tucked it in my purse.

Even though my memories of being pregnant are special to me, I doubt if Jack will appreciate his own prenatal adventures. Besides, after hearing the ultrasound story he'll want to crawl under the pulpit and hide.

Another idea for my ceremonial address is to share my first experience of mother-child separation anxiety. It happened about a decade ago, when I dropped off my little redhead wearing denim overalls on his first day of Jewish preschool. Frankly, I was overcome with emotions after I hesitantly left Jack in the classroom with the teacher and a dozen wandering toddlers. In fact, I ran to the bathroom down the hallway so that I could wipe my mascara-stained face with a piece of cheap toilet paper. Then, I found the nearest telephone, which happened to be in the temple copy room, and called my husband at work.

Me: "I can't believe I abandoned our child with a stranger," I sobbed to Scott on the phone. "The next thing I know Jack will be leaving us to go to college."
Scott: "He'll be fine. Why don't you go check on him before you leave the building?"
Me: "Sure, easy for you to say. You're distracted at the office all day. What am I going to do with myself for the next two hours?"
Scott: "I bet you'll think of something."

Another option is to perform a demonstration speech. For example, I can bring a worn, brown Rawlings glove that Jack wore when he was younger and ask him to squeeze his left hand into the tight leather mitt. (Think OJ Simpson trial.) This visual effect reveals how much he's grown and proves that he's really becoming a man. Now, how many moms have done that?

Perhaps my best bet is to say something more serious and traditional, such as a meaningful quote from the Talmud that was written more than 2,000 years ago. The English text is: "May you live to see your world fulfilled; may you be our link to future worlds; and may your hope encompass all the generations to be. May your heart conceive with understanding; may your mouth speak wisdom and your tongue be stirred with sounds of joy. May your gaze be straight and sure, your eyes be lit with Torah's lamp, your face aglow with heaven's radiance, your lips expressing words of knowledge, and your inner self alive with righteousness. And may you always rush in eagerness to hear the words of One more ancient than all time."

Although the words of the sages are enlightening, I might go with something original and less serious, such as:

Today on your *bar mitzvah*
We are so proud of you.
No one said it's easy
To learn to be a Jew.

Then again, if I feel desperate enough, I can always buy my *bar mitzvah* sentiments over the Internet. That's right, for the bargain price of $19.97, I can purchase a professionally written, customizable, risk-free, not-too-sappy, easy-to-deliver speech that also includes a toast, candle lighting prayer, assorted poems, and God's blessing on the Sabbath. Best of all, this readily available congratulatory speech package is 100 percent guaranteed or my money back.

And I thought nothing in life is guaranteed.

Homemade Strudel Sweetens The *Simcha*

As the big day approaches, my dining room table disappears underneath a hodgepodge of paper goods, *yarmulkes*, party favors, platters, snacks, reply cards, place cards, and so many Judaic items that I'm ready to open up my own gift shop.

However, the most important provision for the *bar mitzvah* party is not on my table but hermetically sealed in heavy-duty aluminum foil in my freezer. I'm talking about the strudel. And anyone who tries to sneak a peak inside the mysterious silver-wrapped shoeboxes that are stacked inside my LG appliance won't live to hear the words *Mazel Tov* ever again.

I'm talking about rows and rows of meticulously packed homemade pastries that, in my opinion, are the sweetest, flakiest, and tastiest treats to land in one's mouth. The strudel to be served at Jack's *bar mitzvah* comes from the loving hands of Great Grandma Ruth and my mom's dear friend Estelle Kent. Over the last several decades, these queens of cuisine have perfected their own strudel recipes and they're the best at hand-stretching the dough until it's thin enough to read a

Sari, age 10, and Great Grandma Ruth, age 89, make strudel, July 2008.

newspaper through. Plus, they don't mind a little flour on their noses when they skillfully work the rolling pin. With much practice, they have mastered the technique of rolling and filling the delicate dough with just the right amount of jelly, raisins, nuts, coconut, and other secret ingredients. (You didn't think I would really give you the recipe, did you?)

When it comes to a Jewish celebration, their strudel dominates the dessert table like a challah on Shabbat or a cantor on the High Holidays.

Recently, I was lucky enough to help (well, mostly observe) Grandma Ruth make strudel for the *bar mitzvah* of her first great grandchild, my son. My job was to grind the pecans while the expert magically flattened each ball of dough on the floured countertop. The sweet, cinnamon aroma filled her little kitchen as I carefully pulled each warped cookie sheet out of the oven. I could hear the crackling of the sizzling hot strawberry, apricot, and pineapple preserves as they melted inside the crisp, golden brown pastry.

Strudel is a German word that literally means "vortex," which doesn't refer to the name of the dough but to the method of rolling the dough around the filling. Most of all, strudel is a Jewish tradition. Other traditions that I have come to cherish are my mother Charlotte's *muhn* cookies and my mother-in-law Vicki's *kamish* bread, which I have yet to try to make, either. It's a Jewish custom to have family and friends bake for a *simcha*, and I'm fortunate to have my own personal baking squad, thanks to the coordination of my special crony Rochelle, who is in charge of assembling all the goodies. When it comes to the love of people you care about, nothing is sweeter. Except maybe ruggalah.

B'nei Mitzvahs Give New Meaning To Tzedkah

Who says kids today are lazy and self-centered? Maybe I did, but never mind. Ask any typical, hormonal, pimply pre-teen preparing for a *bar* or *bat mitzvah* and he or she will show you the contrary. Consider, for example, the relentless demands on Jewish 13-year-olds who are about to embark on symbolic adulthood. To start with, they diligently practice their Torah portion, study their *Haftarah*, write a personal interpretation of the weekly Torah portion, and put up with their mothers who obsess for a whole year over everything from the guest list to the dessert table.

In addition, they're required to chant the *V'ahavta* and several other Hebrew prayers like a trained soprano, only with a cracking pubescent voice in front of a live audience that includes their middle school buddies. On top of that, they must also master the art of public speaking and compose an eloquent speech that makes their already emotionally charged albeit proud mother sob uncontrollably in the front row and cause further embarrassment in front of their friends. From a parent's perspective, *b'nei mitzvah* participants have more on their plates than hungry truck drivers at Old Country Buffet.

Yes, it's hard to imagine how a seventh grader can stand before a congregation in confidence and lead a Shabbat morning service when he isn't even old enough to drive a car and still doesn't make his own bed. Yet with a little guidance from the rabbis and tutor, the majority of *b'nei mitzvah* students manage to rise to the occasion and meet the challenges set before them by their religious ancestors thousands of years ago.

These goals are inscribed in *Pirke Avot*, which means, "The world stands upon three things: Torah, Worship, and Acts of Loving Kindness."

These three pillars sum up the requirement to become a *bar* and *bat mitzvah*, and they are the foundation of *b'nei mitzvah* programs at congregations nationwide. Unlike in any other religion, the *b'nei mitzvah* experience gives young Jewish people the privileged opportunity to be a role model to their peers and discover their own strengths and uniqueness. And when they read from the Torah for the first time, the ceremony itself represents a beginning, not an end, to their Jewish journey.

The *b'nei mitzvah* celebration is indeed the best time to demonstrate their individuality and lifelong commitment to do their part in making the world a better place, or *tikkun olam*. That's right, in their spare time, *bar* and *bat mitzvah* students are required to choose their own social action causes that make a difference in the lives of others through acts of loving kindness.

Again, sounds like way too much to handle when this age group is already overloaded with schoolwork, sports, extracurricular activities, and more places to be than a Hannah Montana tour bus. Even so, the new generation of *b'nei mitzvah* students knows how to get the job done. They're bright, outspoken, multi-dimensional, creative, caring, and hard working, to say the least. Likewise, their concept of *tzedakah* includes more than collecting money for a random charity. In fact, the biggest question they face, other than how many presents they'll get, is which social justice project is right for them.

Meaningful *Mitzvahs* Are A Big Hit WithTeens

Mitzvah projects are as unique as the Hebrew school students themselves, and it's hard to say who benefits the most, the giver or the receiver. With a keen awareness of social justice and diverse skills and interests, today's young Jewish people are eager to choose a *tzedakah* project that goes beyond collecting money for a charity.

Mitzvah projects are most meaningful when they help people help themselves. For example, Heifer International (www.heifer. org) is a non-profit organization whose goal is to help end world hunger and poverty through self-reliance and sustainability. For example, $120 buys a sheep in Peru; $150 pays for a llama in Ecuador; and $250 covers a water buffalo in Asia, which allows poor villagers across the globe to earn their own livelihoods and produce their own food.

Perhaps the most powerful *b'nei mitzvah* experience is when kids make a difference to other kids. For example, when my son Jack first started looking for his *mitzvah* project, he knew for sure that he wanted to combine his love of baseball and help kids less fortunate than him. He chose to be a "buddy" through an organization called St. Louis Challenger Baseball, which allows youngsters and adults with developmental disabilities to play the popular sport. Now in its 14th year and with teams throughout

St. Louis, this special baseball league enables everyone to be a winner.

During baseball season, Jack helps motivate players with physical and/or mental challenges to experience the excitement of a real ballgame. The social interaction between the players and the volunteers is hard to beat. At a recent game, Jack helped 8-year-old Matthew hold a plastic bat and together they tapped the ball. With the crowd cheering, Jack hustled as he pushed Matthew in his wheelchair to first base. Then, Jack kneeled down to lift up Matthew's oversized baseball cap and uncovered his eyeglasses so that the beaming boy on base could see all the action. Jack patted Matthew's tiny shoulder and told him, "Good job buddy!"

At another game at Ranken-Jordan, a pediatric specialty hospital in St. Louis, Jack scooped up a grounder that slowly rolled to him in the outfield and then quickly placed the baseball in Matthew's glove. The next inning, Jack dropped a ball on purpose to allow enthusiastic 21-year-old Libby with Down syndrome to make an exciting home run followed by a standing ovation and lots of applause.

"Baseball is a great sport, and every kid who wants to play should have the chance to play," said Jack. "I feel good when I can encourage the kids to hit the ball and make it around the bases every inning, even if they aren't physically able to swing the bat and run by themselves. We all have a fun time."

The social action project is a great opportunity for *bar* and *bat mitzvah* students to make a difference in the world, one person or animal at a time.

Bar Mitzvah Brings Everyone Closer

By the time you read this, Jack's *bar mitzvah* will be over. No more sleepless nights playing musical chairs with seating charts. For more than a year now, I've been writing about this upcoming Jewish milestone in my son's life. What am I going to talk about now—*matzo brei?*

I'm not old enough to be the parent of a teenager, especially one who is wearing a designer suit, silk tie, and a beautiful *tallis* and *yarmulke* that his Aunt Cher needle-pointed especially for him in honor of his *bar mitzvah.* As my son stands at the pulpit and proudly holds the Torah scrolls, I'm in awe. He carefully follows the hand-scribed Hebrew text with a brand new ornate silver *yad* that his preschool friend Nicolette has given him just a few days before his *bar mitzvah.* At that moment, it's a privilege to be a Jew, especially when you consider that the Torah was written 974 generations, or 2,000 years, before the world was created.

The *bar mitzvah* journey, at least for me, is something that has brought me closer to Judaism. Every holiday becomes more meaningful. When my children ask the Four Questions at the Passover seder this year, they relive their Jewish history, much like at a *bar mitzvah.* Participating in the prayer service, reciting blessings over the Torah reading, and chanting the *Haftarah*, is something that I don't take for granted anymore. It takes a lot of work for a 13-year-old boy or girl to become a *bar* or *bat mitzvah.* It also takes a lot of gas mileage getting to Hebrew school twice a week, but let's not go there.

After my son gives his speech and thanks his mom and dad "for always being there" for him, I can't help but think he really means it. Then again, the rabbi told him to say so. Seriously, the *bar mitzvah* brings us all closer to our family and our faith, and that's what being Jewish is all about.

I never thought I would say this but I'm speechless at this point. Now is a good time for a silent meditation.

The Gift Of Disconnection

If there's one thing I learned at Jack's *bar mitzvah*, besides never wear new high heels without breaking them in first, is that I can't control some things in life. For example, I can't control the weather and whether the rain will allow Jack's baseball friends to attend his party. Also, I can't control the health of people and whether they will be sick or well enough to physically be there for this special time in my son's life.

It's hard for me to give up control and not worry about every little thing. So when my phone suddenly stops working for two whole days during the *bar mitzvah* weekend and I can't retrieve or identify any of the endless ringing calls, I feel helpless and frustrated. That's when I realize that I'm better off not knowing any last minute changes and just trust that everything will be okay.

Hmmmm, sounds like a metaphor for something more significant.

Even though my phone malfunction is inconvenient at the time, I appreciate the disconnection from any outside distractions. All I can do now is focus on the moment and not whether the caterer ordered enough tablecloths. Perhaps the telephone trouble is divine intervention from God or maybe another screw up with Charter Communications. Doesn't matter. I get the hint.

Like the red and white helium balloons that gradually float down from my dining room ceiling, so do I. I've been on a high for so long and now that the *bar mitzvah* is over, I'm slowly exhaling and coming back down to the ground. I'm not holding my breath any more in anticipation of the big day. It feels so good to have special memories of the *bar mitzvah* ceremony and celebration. Most importantly, my son has added another link in our Jewish heritage, and his commitment to study Torah is stronger than ever.

Finally, I can relax and not think about organizing any big events for awhile.

Then again, Sari's *bat mitzvah* is scheduled for 2011. So I better start planning now.

Photos Speak A Thousand Words

I don't consider myself a procrastinator, unless, of course, the chore has something to do with cleaning out the freezer. When I have a job to do, I get it done. Usually.

For example, my son asks me to find him a girdle to wear at football practice. Done. Sari requests a kosher salami sandwich with mayonnaise in her school lunch. Done. My

I embarrass Jack, while Sari laughs and Scott has his eyes closed, March 2008. *(photo by Don Siegel)*

husband's trousers are ready for pickup at the dry cleaners. Done. The dog needs a haircut. Done. I have to write a story on the benefits of Torah yoga. Done.

One thing I can't seem to get done is my son's *bar mitzvah* photo album.

For some reason, the final selection of which pictures go on which page, not to mention the sizes and quantities, eludes me. Even though Jack's *bar mitzvah* was in March, almost a half year ago, I have yet to make any final decisions. Besides, I can't find enough space to hang the 20 x 24 wall portrait of Jack wearing a *tallis* unless I remove my flat screen TV over the mantle. The other option is to build an addition to my home so that I can display as many framed memories as I want over the years. I will call it the "*simcha* room."

So much time has passed that relatives no longer ask for their reprints. I rationalize to the grandparents that their 13-year-old grandson doesn't look the same anyway. Besides, they can enjoy the larger-than-life photo cutout of Jack, which is leftover from his *bar mitzvah* party and still proudly stands in my foyer. The enormous foam board cutout of Jack outfitted in his red-striped baseball uniform scares everyone who enters through the front door, but it's a great conversation piece nonetheless.

Perhaps one reason that I struggle with the *bar mitzvah* album, which is now upgraded to a stylish coffee table book, is because my husband's eyes are closed in practically every pose. In fact, Scott's eyelids are either shut completely or hang droopy as if he just woke up from a nap and wears a handsome tailored suit instead of boxer shorts. He explains to me that his natural reflex causes him to blink whenever he sees a flashbulb. So why do the rabbis never seem to have that problem and they're in front of the cameras all the time?

Fortunately, our professional photographer can fix these goof ups. With the latest digital technology, Scott eyes can magically open. Then again, his hazel eyes now appear with a tiny black dot that resembles a pencil doodle in a high school yearbook. Lucky for me, the same camera wizardry also can erase double chins.

Bottom line, nothing tells a story better than a photograph, including the annual picture of Jack and Sari standing next to our willow tree on their first day of school. With their backpacks strapped over their shoulders, they usually complain, "Why are you taking our picture again? You did the same thing last year."

Exactly. Maybe my children don't appreciate it now, but I'm always trying to capture time. I can't help but notice how the weeping branches in our backyard grow bigger every year, just like Jack and Sari. Indeed, a picture says a thousand words, even when my husband's eyes are closed.

Bar Mitzvah Memories

It's hard to believe that a year has passed since Jack's *bar mitzvah* and my son is one year closer to his driver's permit. Since his passage into adulthood, I seem to have more time on my hands. No more countless hours spent on rehearsing speeches and *aliyahs*, playing musical chairs with the seating chart, driving to tutor sessions, and making life or death decisions, such as whether to serve chicken or sirloin kabobs at the *kiddish* luncheon. No longer are my days filled with digging out baby pictures for the musical slide show, editing typos in the *bar mitzvah* program, shopping for dress shoes, designing table centerpieces, picking out party favors, and testing my willpower to not sneak a piece of homemade strudel from the freezer.

To be honest, I don't miss any of that. Well, maybe the strudel. What I do miss is listening to Jack eloquently chant *teffilah* with his bedroom door closed when he doesn't know I'm standing there. To this day, I get goose bumps when I hear the gentle melody of the *Avot v'imahot* and the Hebrew names of our ancestors: "*Ehlohei Abraham, ehlohei Yitzchak, veilohei Yaakov,*

Ehlohei Sarah, ehlohei Rivkah, ehlohei Leiah, veilohei Racheil..."
When Jack sings these prayers, he unites his soul with Jews
everywhere in the world. Now I get it.

To help preserve the memories of Jack's *bar mitzvah*, I've saved
memorabilia, from a stack of *Mazel Tov* cards to assorted colored
yarmulkes monogrammed with the names of his friends, in a big
plastic storage box that I keep in my closet. I realize that Jack
might not care what's inside the box right now, but maybe one
day when he has a son or daughter of his own he'll treasure the
blue binder with Cantor Seth's scribbled notes in the margin
that say, "Jack—Go sit down! You were awesome!" Jack also
might have a good laugh when he sees the silly photo of him and
his friends, who are eating melted Ted Drewes frozen custard in
front of a stretch limousine.

Most importantly, when he digs through the plastic container,
he'll rediscover many special things that will serve him
throughout his life, including his very own *tallis* and *yarmulke*
that his Aunt Cher needle-pointed with a swirling design of
blue, black, gold, and silver threads. Even the tiny box of "pocket
blessings" hidden inside a red pouch may help guide him or give
him the inspiration he needs for that moment in time.

As our family approaches the *bimah* on the one-year anniversary
of Jack's *bar mitzvah*, I can't help but get a tear in my eye. Maybe
because Sari and I are privileged to light the temple's Shabbat
candles together. Maybe because the skirt that I wore last year
is now two sizes too small and pinches my waistline. Or maybe
because I'm filled with pride again as Jack stands in front of the
congregation and reads with confidence his Torah portion.

I feel blessed. And I feel nervous. Sari's *bat mitzvah* is scheduled
for November 2011. I better buy another box.

A Parent's Guide To *Bar/Bat Mitzvah* Planning

If there's one thing I learned from Jack's *bar mitzvah*, it is try not to stress over the small stuff, because when it's over all that's left are wonderful memories and a box full of satin monogrammed *kippots.* Actually, a parent's job pales in comparison to the enormous responsibilities of Jewish adolescents studying for a *bar* or *bat mitzvah.* These pubescent souls are required to learn Hebrew, memorize prayers, interpret lessons of the sages, stand before the congregation and lead the service, master the art of public speaking, and repair the world doing *b'nei mitzvah* projects while they keep up with schoolwork, extracurricular activities, and orthodontic appointments. On top of that, they're expected to crank out legible and poetic thank you notes faster than a stenographer.

During this incredibly busy time, parents must remember what really matters, and that is for their teen to work hard, have fun, and be proud of their accomplishments. Hopefully, the following tips will help you make your child's *bar* or *bat mitzvah* a joyful experience.

Step 1: Plan as much as you can in advance. Synagogues assign *bar* and *bat mitzvah* dates several years ahead so there's no excuse to wait until the last minute. By the time your child graduates from preschool you're ready to book the location where the service and party will be held, such as at a temple, hotel, recreation center, or Western Wall in Jerusalem. If you have more than one child, hopefully their ages are spaced far enough apart so that you can recoup your finances.

Traditionally, a *bar* or *bat mitzvah* should be scheduled close to the child's birthday; however, if your son or daughter has a winter birthday, consider bumping the date ahead to springtime or move it behind to autumn when the weather is nicer. Then again, you can't control the weather, and it can pour buckets any time of year. Besides, rain on a Jewish *simcha* brings good luck.

Step 2: Set a budget for the celebration and be prepared to blow it on hidden costs of helium balloons, monogrammed party favors, tablecloth rentals, customized postage stamps, bus transportation to and from the party, motivational dancers, glow-in-the-dark necklaces, personalized programs, and, of course, a deluxe chocolate fountain.

Step 3: At least one year in advance, nab the photographer, videographer, and DJ before the mother of your child's best friend does. Also, make hotel accommodations for out of town guests and inquire about discounts to reserve a block of rooms. Many people like to mail save-the-date notices to important family and friends, especially those who travel from another state. To thank them for spending thousands of dollars on this occasion in honor of your son or daughter, the least you can do is welcome them with a goody bag that might include a variety of snacks, souvenirs, a weekend itinerary, driving directions, important contact numbers, and maps to St. Louis landmarks, such as the Arch and abandoned Chrysler plant.

Step 4: Stay organized at all times. Use a database to keep track of everything, including an updated list of RSVPs, menu, prices, seating chart, vendors, mailing labels, and a description of the gifts received from your guests so that you know how much to spend on them when their event rolls around.

Step 5: Involve your child in some of the decision making, such as the theme of the party and design of the invitations. Then do what you want anyway because, after all, you're paying the bills. Keep in mind that adolescents constantly change their minds and their friends come and go like pimples.

Step 6: Ask a friend who owes you a favor to coordinate the

baking of cookies and sweets for your dessert table. And go easy on the *kamish* bread. Kids still like brownies the best. Most importantly, ration out the homemade strudel so that you have plenty for yourself to savor when you get home.

Step 7: Stock up on Best Buy gift cards now—the same way you hoard tubs of Cool Whip when they go on sale. If your son or daughter is invited to more than one party on the same day, good luck. It takes experienced coordination and precise timing, not to mention a full tank of gas, to get your teen across town for services, *oneg* receptions, luncheons, dinners, dancing, and laser tag, but it can be done.

Step 8: If you want to entertain your crowd with a musical slide show, get your photos organized as soon as possible. When digging out those baby snapshots don't forget to include poses of your child with every single member of the immediate family so that no one's feelings are hurt. Try to keep the production under 12 minutes. As sentimental as the photo montage is to you, your fidgety guests are there to eat cake and shuffle to the electric slide. Nobody else really cares about pictures of your spaghetti-stained toddler wearing diapers.

Step 9: Keep your speeches short and try not to sob uncontrollably. Your son or daughter is embarrassed enough as it is.

Step 10: Think twice before ordering a poster-sized canvas portrait of your pimply-faced adolescent wearing braces and hugging the Torah because he or she will look totally different by the time you mount the frame on the wall.

Step 11: Finally, enjoy this exciting time that you've worked so hard to put together and choreograph from start to finish. Let yourself go, but don't do anything stupid at the party because your mug might end up on Facebook the next day.

Chapter 10
School Daze

Middot Makes The Grade

Academic success is driven into the brains of our children before they tinkle in their first diaper. Although there's no concrete scientific evidence that education begins in the womb, a hormonal pregnant woman will do just about anything to give her growing fetus the best start in life. It's not unheard of for an expectant mother to play Mozart to her swollen belly. The hope is that exposure to classical music will increase the likelihood of giving birth to a musical protégé who can play *Chopsticks* and suck on a pacifier at the same time.

When a parent brings the bundle of joy home from the hospital, the sleepy newborn is greeted with more black and white abstract images than a Rorschach inkblot test at a psychiatrist's office. Before the infant can balance his wobbly head, he is plopped in a bouncy seat in front of the television. The exhausted mom dozes on the couch while the toothless viewer watches *Baby Einstein* videos that stimulate the brain to eventually operate a DVD player and hold a sippy cup simultaneously. Even when away from home and on the road, the curious tot is strapped in a car seat and watches the latest Disney release or stares straight ahead at a blurry mirror and dizzying pictures of bull's eyes that are attached to the back of the driver's headrest.

Parents mean well, but it could be that our intellectual demands are the reason why some toddlers give up naps. Nobody snoozes in nursery school anymore, except maybe the teachers, and, besides, a nursery refers to the place at the maternity ward anyway. Nowadays, preschools, also known as early education centers, boast as many computers as they do wooden blocks. To stay ahead of the competition, many pre-kindergarten programs offer foreign language classes as well. When Sari attended Jewish preschool, in fact, she learned more Spanish than Hebrew.

By the time kindergarten actually rolls around, many children can count to 10 in Spanish and in sign language, but they'd rather log onto a computer than print their names. By first grade, students dive right into spelling tests, oral book presentations, and state-required assessment tests that drag on through high school. After Sari's first week of second grade, she came home from elementary school with a painful callus on her finger because she gripped a No. 2 pencil too long. The standardized tests are so boring, in fact, that students give them nicknames; my kids call the Comprehensive Test of Basic Skills (the CTBS) "Child Torture Before Summer."

Then comes middle school and an onslaught of "challenge" courses, pimples, mood swings, cell phones, and, sooner or later, a tutor for college-entrance exams. In high school, teenagers push themselves to graduate magna cum laude, get into an Ivy League college, and gain a competitive edge in the workforce before they even nail their first summer internship. After all, if they want to decorate their dorm room like a Pottery Barn catalog, someone has to pay for it.

In my opinion, scholastic achievement is overrated. Many parents put way too much pressure on their children, from preschool to post graduation. Kids are stressed out, and so are parents. I don't reward Jack and Sari for perfect report cards and I don't take away a privilege if they bring home something less. I expect them to do their best. I also expect them to make mistakes and learn from them.

Sure, good grades are important, but book smarts alone won't get young people very far in life if they lack common sense and social skills. Fortunately, many public and private schools across the country have implemented "character education" in their new and improved curriculums. Students learn how to identify and strengthen their own positive traits, such as responsibility, respect, perseverance, patience, and citizenship that are essential in today's society.

Character education may be a sign of the times, but the idea of building desirable traits is actually old Jewish wisdom. In fact, Judaism has a word for it—*middot*—which literally means measures or qualities that bring us closer to God. Although the classroom provides an excellent opportunity for children to learn universal values and ethical behavior, the Jewish sages stress that the real teachers are the parents who provide moral guidance at home.

My kids practice *middot* everyday without even knowing it. When Jack finds someone's homework on a desk and turns it into the teacher, he demonstrates *middot*, or kindness. When he resists beating up his sister after she teases him, he shows *middot*, or self-control. When Sari blocks the soccer ball from the goalie net, she exercises *middot*, or courage. When she puts away the sidewalk chalk and bikes in the garage without being asked, she exemplifies *middot*, or responsibility.

When it comes to *middot*, the homework is never done. *Middot* is a lifelong lesson in compassion, truth, diligence, peace of mind, humility, and other positive attributes that help us to become better Jews.

When Average Is Just Right

As far as careers go, I could never be an elementary school teacher. I just don't have the patience, nor do I have any desire to inspire on a daily basis an overheated classroom of two-dozen rambunctious children, many of whom use their sleeves to wipe their noses. If I never do another *mitzvah* again, at least I can say that I've proudly dedicated many hours as a tireless room mother for the past decade, and still counting.

Thank God for teachers, at least the good ones, because they stimulate thinking and motivate young people to learn. In Judaism, parents and teachers are one and the same and education goes way beyond the classroom. When it comes to Jewish studies, the Torah is our textbook. In Deuteronomy, the sages tell us, "You shall teach them diligently unto your children…and speak of them when you sit in your home, when you walk by the way, in your lying down, and in your rising up."

This sounds like a lot of work on our part. I mean, think about all the lessons the Torah gives us about our religion, values, culture, language, and traditions handed down for thousands of years, not to mention a whole other world of *midrash* to explore underneath all that Hebrew text.

Sure, God gives us a lot of homework to study in a single lifetime, but it still doesn't compare to the heavy workload and paperwork involved at a single parent-teacher conference. All kidding aside, teachers today are overworked and underappreciated. And my guess is that one of the least favorite parts of their occupation, aside from disciplining troublemakers and occasionally eating blah cafeteria food, is the physical and mental preparation required for the annual parent-teacher conferences.

But enough about the sufferings of a teacher—what about the moms and dads who are forced to squat on those little plastic chairs that have wads of bubble gum stuck to the bottom? Even though I approach each educational encounter with confidence and always walk away feeling proud, I still get a little tongue-tied when I come face-to-face with the person who spends more time with my child than I do some days. Even now, I dread when I stumble over the word "synonym," which usually comes out of my mouth sounding like "cinnamon."

Twice a year, I look forward to these 15-minute time slots with my child's teacher because I usually get to scurry (somebody's vocabulary word for the week) out of the house without doing the dishes. Still, I admit that I feel a tinge of nervousness when I discuss the genius qualities of my children with anyone outside of my own immediate family. After all, I take full credit for any satisfactory marks when it comes to grammar, punctuation, and correct pencil grip.

I always remember one of the first parent-teacher conferences that Scott and I attended because I learned a valuable lesson: never underestimate the time you'll spend at school that evening because at least one other mom will chat endlessly about the apple of her eye. Even though this particularly significant meeting with Jack's first grade teacher happened over five years ago, I remember our conversation like it was yesterday.

Scott and I patiently waited our turn in the hallway along with the other fidgety parents who lined up against the wall as if we were in detention outside the principal's office. Eventually, we all got bored and paced the corridors, twiddled our thumbs, and smacked our gum until another name was called. Once in a while, a mom would have a meltdown because she was afraid that her six-year-old son wasn't reading fast enough and would be held back a year. (Not that I'd ever eavesdrop on a private conversation.)

Finally, it was our turn to visit with Jack's teacher, whom I'll call "Mrs. M." Everyone adored Mrs. M., whose genuinely warm smile was contagious and her fashionable outfits to die for. She was truly passionate about teaching, and her many years of experience gave her complete control over her students. I wish I could say the same about my own parenting skills.

To my recollection, our therapy session, I mean parent-teacher conference, went something like this:

Mrs. M.: "Jack is such a pleasure to have in class. He gets along with everyone. He is a hard worker and he is very bright. I love his red hair."
Me: "Thank you."
Mrs. M.: "As you can see from his spelling test, he got four out of five words correct, which is very good."
Me: "Now, wait a minute. He has all the right letters—w-n-a-t. They're just not in the right order."
Mrs. M.: "Exactly."
Me: "So what does this mean? Does he need a spelling tutor?"
Mrs. M.: "Of course not. He is meeting expectations in all of his subjects, except he can work a little harder on capitalization."
Me: "I'll get right on that!"
Mrs. M.: "In reading, he blends consonant sounds and short vowels in monosyllabic words."

Me: "Is that a good thing?"

Mrs.: M.: "In math, he scores in the 97th percentile."

Scott: "Jack is good with numbers. He gets that from me."

Mrs. M.: "Here's a picture of hearts and arrows that he drew for you. It says, 'I love my mommy.' Isn't that sweet?"

Me: "Can you please pass the tissues? I get a little emotional."

Mrs. M.: "I am very proud of the progress that Jack has made this year. He is a perfectly..."

Me: "Thank..."

Mrs. M.: "...average student."

Me: "What? Did you say average? I thought you told me that he was doing so well."

Mrs. M.: "He is doing excellent and is a very well-rounded boy with strengths and weaknesses that are to be expected. As a parent and a teacher, I couldn't ask for anything more."

On that note, we shook hands with Mrs. M. and said goodbye. Then we went home and hugged our little guy who waited up for us, of course. "What did my teacher say about me?" Jack asked curiously as he laid on his pillow.

With a tear still in my eye, I calmly answered him, "Your teacher says that you are a perfectly average student. Keep up the good work. We couldn't be more proud of you."

In the end, the most important lesson that I learned that day is the same one that Judaism reinforces in The Book of Proverbs: "Teach a child *bed'arko*, or in the way he should go." To me, this means that a child learns in his own unique way and at his own pace. A child should learn for the sake of learning and not for a statistic on a photocopied slip of paper or for the satisfaction of his parents. A child's intelligence is therefore measured by how he applies his knowledge to improve his life and better his world.

Children Are On Loan From God

Some parents live vicariously through their children. When it comes to their kid's success, some moms and dads take it personally. When it comes to their child's failures, they take that personally, too. I guess some parents figure that if they didn't get it right the first time, that is, in their own childhood, then surely they can get another shot at perfection when they raise their son or daughter. In our competitive society, a parent's expectations are higher than ever, and these pressures seem to start at a younger age all the time.

Moreover, you can spot these kinds of neurotic moms and dads miles away, whether at the neighborhood ball field, holiday dance recital, middle school spelling bee, or wherever else parents tend to put their protégés on pedestals.

For example, the assistant baseball coach wearing the Cardinals cap is a wanna-be-major-leaguer who nervously chews sunflower seeds and paces behind the chain link fence every time his own 8-year-old steps up to the plate. When his little slugger strikes out, guess who's having the temper tantrum? As the dad spits out a wad of broken shells, he follows his defeated son to the dugout to dish out even more humiliation.

Likewise, an anxious stage mom futzes with her four-year-old daughter's pink tutu and sparkly lip gloss right before the curtain rises. The mother finally takes a seat in the audience and turns on the video camera, only to capture her precious preschooler twirling across the stage in the wrong direction and innocently knocking into another little ballerina with matching hair ribbons. The embarrassed mother is horrified as the giggling dancers collapse like dominoes on stage. The following week, she switches her daughter to gymnastics.

As far as scholastic achievement, parental pressure is always on. For example, at a spelling bee, fidgety parents sit in the front row in the gymnasium and mumble letters under their breath. When their straight-A student leans into the squeaky microphone on stage and spells out words like, s-c-h-i-z-o-p-h-r-e-n-i-a, it feels like a diagnosis has been made. With each new word, the grownups catch their breath again and give their child a thumbs up as the youngster moves to the next round of competition.

When it comes to Jewish parenting, in particular, we really know how to lay on the guilt. Jewish comedian Joel Chasnoff illustrates this point beautifully. Growing up, he jokes that his mother had a bumper sticker on her car that read, "If my son worked just a little bit harder, I, too, would have an honor roll student at Jefferson High School."

Actually, Jewish wisdom has another approach on how to raise children to become successful adults. Basically, the sages advise parents to chill out and let young people find their own way. In other words, according to a Hasidic teaching, "If your child has a talent to be a baker, don't ask him to be a doctor."

Not only that, Judaism emphasizes that our offspring don't even belong to us in the first place. Instead, God loans our children to us like everything else we hold so dear. Our job is to guide our children in a holy direction. In the process, maybe we parents will learn something.

Virginia Tech: Sadness, Strength & Suffering

Once again, our nation mourns. This time we grieve and struggle to understand last week's bloody rampage at Virginia Tech, where 33 lives were abruptly ended. One of the victims was Livio Librescu, an engineering professor and Holocaust survivor, who lived through the atrocities of the concentration camps as a little boy, but not the horror that struck more than 60 years later at his workplace turned war zone. In one of life's cruel, twisted ironies, Librescu died a hero on *Yom HaShoah*, the international day of remembrance for victims of the Holocaust. On that tragic Monday morning at a typically peaceful college campus, the Romanian immigrant gave his life to save the lives of others. To protect the students in his classroom, the courageous 76-year-old husband and father barricaded the door with his body and was consequently riddled with bullets by the 23-year-old psychopathic gunman on the other side.

As so many stories of heroism and bravery continue to unfold, the massacre at Virginia Tech serves as an opportunity to teach our children how human strength prevails in the depths of despair and suffering. At the same time, this new generation of weapons-savvy terrorists reminds parents that our children are no longer safe at school. My gut reaction is to protect Jack and Sari from learning about the catastrophe at Virginia Tech, but my attempts to shield them from reality are short lived.

When the shocking news first broke, I tried to take in as much of the media frenzy as possible before my kids returned home from school. The ugly mug of Don Imus disappeared off the front pages and was replaced by videos of SWAT teams and mangled students being carried out of buildings. I can barely comprehend the events of this mass murder that unfold before my eyes on CNN, so how can I expect my kids to begin to understand? Sure, this latest killing spree brutally justifies the routine intruder drills that my kids practice at school, but I still want to shield them from the violence and cruelty that exists out there. I don't want them to worry about things over which they have no control. I still want them to go to school every day without feeling paranoid.

So I quickly turn off the television news when I hear Jack plow through the door and fling his backpack and tennis shoes in the laundry room. My sixth-grader plops down on the couch next to me and we talk about his day.

Me: "How was school?"
Jack: "Good."
Me: "How was gym?"
Jack: "Good."
Me: "How was lunch?"
Jack: "Good."
Me: What kind of homework do you have today?"
Jack: "Good."

Then my son interrupts our stimulating conversation with:

Jack: "Did you hear about the student killings in Virginia?"
Me: "Uhh, yes, actually, I've been watching the news on television. It's a terrible thing that happened. What do you know about it?"
Jack: "Our principal handed out a note to everyone."
Me: "What's it say?"

Jack digs through crumpled pieces of paper and hands me a letter from the school superintendent. It explains that in the aftermath of the devastating tragedy at Virginia Tech, school safety remains a priority and counselors and other resources are available if students or parents want to discuss their fears or concerns. Before I have a chance to ask Jack another question, he races upstairs to play on the computer. By the time he comes back downstairs for a chocolate chip cookie and glass of milk, the Internet has already informed him about the latest details of the senseless and ruthless shooting spree.

Our discussion picks up from where we left off.

Me: "So how do you feel about the school shooting?"

Jack: "Good."

Me: "Come on, Jack, how do you feel good?"

Jack: "I mean that I feel sorry for the people who died and were hurt. I think the shooter is crazy. But I still feel safe at my school."

While both Jack and Sari process the chilling facts in bite-size pieces and at their own pace, I call their attention to the peaceful community that comes together in its sorrow. I want Jack and Sari to appreciate how the families and friends of the victims lean on each other, as well as their faith, to help them cope and heal in the painful years ahead.

During the university-wide convocation that took place on the day after the worst mass murder in America, representatives of different religious groups, from Muslims to Jews, share their insights about life and death and God.

For thousands of years, Jewish thinkers have explored the topic of good and evil and Kohelet's words of wisdom in the biblical book of Ecclesiastes still make sense today. He wrote:

1. To every thing there is a season, and a time to every purpose under the heaven:

2. A time to be born, and a time to die; a time to plant, and a time to plug up that which is planted;

3. A time to kill, and a time to heal; a time to break down, and a time to build up;

4. A time to weep, and a time to laugh; a time to mourn, and a time to dance;

5. A time to cast away stones, and a time to gather stones together; a time to embrace and a time to refrain from embracing;

6. A time to seek, and a time to lose; a time to keep, and a time to cast away;

7. A time to rend, and a time to sew; a time to keep silence, and a time to speak;

8. A time to love, and a time to hate; a time for war, and a time for peace.

Too Much Self-Esteem For Generation Me

Every generation has an alias. The grandparents of the Baby Boomers are called the post-Civil War Missionary Generation. The parents of the Boomers are labeled the Lost Generation or the G.I. Generation, which fought in World War II and survived the Depression. They created the next population explosion of ambitious movers and shakers and anti-war protestors, the Baby Boomers, which, in turn, introduced Generation Jones.

Stick with me here. The demographics get even more confusing. Next comes the spiritual awakening in American history known as the Consciousness Revolution, followed by the ambiguous Generation Xers and the pop culture influences of the MTV Generation, Boomerang Generation, and Generation Y.

Furthermore, market researchers characterize children born between 1982 and 2000 as the Millennials and they are a sub-category of the New Silent Generation, also called Generation Z. In summary, someone please explain to me who I am and who my children are supposed to be.

What concerns me most is that the population that was born since the 1980s during the so-called "self-esteem movement" has earned yet another distinction: Generation Me. According to psychiatrists who research this sort of thing, today's college students are more self-centered than any generation in history as a result of our misguided notion that self-esteem makes a child happier, brighter, and more successful.

Based on a study called the Narcissistic Personality Inventory, which evaluated the changing attitudes of college students from 1982 to 2006, high self-esteem may be to blame for this generation of egomaniacs that is about to enter the workforce and shape our future. Of course, there's always exceptions to such sweeping generalizations, as evidenced by the college students who sacrificed their own needs and took care of each other in the aftermath of the recent Virginia Tech massacre.

Still, many children who are now coming of age favor personal gain over contributing to the greater good. True, volunteerism is on the rise, but that's most likely because some schools recommend community service on a resume, much like a *mitzvah* project is required for Hebrew school students. Perhaps because of society's high expectations, most graduates feel the pressure to jumpstart their careers rather than take time off to teach children in Equador how to read.

This alarming trend of narcissism flourishes on school playgrounds, as well as college campuses. For more than two decades, parents, educators, and therapists have been programmed to believe that high self-esteem and praise are good for children and that the more special they feel about themselves the better. Truth is, high self-esteem has little to do with improved academic or job performance, nor does feeling good about oneself prevent underage smoking, drinking, crime, and inappropriate sexual activity. Young people may seem more confident on the outside, but on the inside they feel miserable because their self-worth is based on external reinforcement.

The National Association for Self-Esteem (yes, really) defines self-esteem simply as the experience of being capable of meeting life's challenges and feeling worthy of happiness. While self-esteem is important to healthy development, boosting a child's ego with phony praise does more harm than good.

Exaggerated acclaim starts early and innocently enough, such as when a preschooler scribbles a purple line on a piece of paper and the proud parent is quick to hang it on the refrigerator door. Think about it—how many times in a single day do we tell our kids, "Way to go!" and "Good job!" and "Awesome!" even when that means they put their dishes in the sink, blow their nose, or get the mail for us. Big deal.

It seems that all a kid has to do these days to earn a pat on the back is wake up for school. "Thanks for rolling out of bed so easily this morning, honey. You're a real trooper!" Or, how about, "At least you tried to clean up your room, so here's an allowance for effort."

Even when the soccer team comes in last place, they still get a trophy. By the time a typical teenager gets her driver's license, she has more colorful ribbons, fancy certificates, and bogus awards shoved in her desk drawer than a Nobel Peace Prize winner and Olympic athlete combined.

Parents want to protect their children from disappointment, but this type of flattery gives children a false sense of security. At the first hint of criticism, they crumble. When they face rejection or failure, they become aggressive or even violent. Maintaining relationships is a struggle.

Well-deserved recognition for worthy accomplishments is one thing, but empty praise for ordinary tasks is meaningless. When a first grader turns in her spelling words, for example, she gets to choose between a Tootsie Roll and taffy in the big glass jar. When a fifth grader fills out a reading slip, she wins a gift certificate to Pizza Hut. When a middle schooler raises her grade point average, she earns ice cream at a school assembly. Are we raising a smarter generation or a fatter one?

Judaism has a better approach to boost self-esteem. In addition to authoritative parenting, children benefit most when they are helping others through *mitzvot*, or sacred good deeds. In the aftermath of the Virginia Tech mass shooting, many students and faculty seek counseling, while others put their intense emotions into action on behalf of the victims who lost their lives. They rally together to make the campus safer and they comfort each other through participation in memorials, contributions to scholarships, and do anything possible to help the grieving families and keep the memories of their loved ones alive.

The School Supply Olympics

For many parents, shopping for school supplies is a test of endurance requiring mental and physical stamina. On the heels of the summer Olympics, I can't help but compare this competitive back-to-school ritual to an athletic race.

Picture this: Teams of children and their moms in running shoes take their marks at the store entrance. When the whistle blows, they grab their carts and sprint to the school supply aisle located strategically next to the Halloween candy.

Racers break into a sweat as they lunge for hole reinforcers, zippered pencil pouches, protractors, and other items in accordance to strict regulations on the supply list. For example, points are deducted for grabbing college-ruled instead of wide-ruled notebook paper. Non-washable markers are grounds for disqualification. All participants must pass a caffeine-free test and be old enough to drive a shopping cart. No coupons are allowed.

Prizes are awarded to the top three teams to cross the checkout line. Third place wins a $50 gift card for the school cafeteria;

second place goes home with a case of Post-it notes; and the gold medal champion wins a year's worth of glue sticks and an unlimited gym pass.

My point is that everything in life seems to move faster these days. It's still August and yet the department store mannequins already wear turtlenecks, while I'm still trying to find the perfect swimsuit. That's why when it comes to school supplies, I waste no time stocking up on spiral notebooks and index cards. I begin my quest for three-ring binders before the first day of summer camp even begins. My intentions are to get better organized, and Jack and Sari share my enthusiasm.

In preparation for his last year of middle school, Jack hoards more mechanical pencils than a graphic design studio. If his enormous collection of lead refills is any indication of how much he plans to study in eighth grade, I won't stop him.

Sari takes her school supplies seriously as well. Now in fourth grade, she scrutinizes over which two-pocket folders have the most adorable pictures of puppies on the cover. Likewise, it takes no less than an hour to choose a new insulated lunch bag that coordinates with her backpack.

Finally, the school year is off to a great start. My kids go to bed earlier. Plus, I listen to whatever music I want when I drive. I also have an excuse to buy mini crackers and bite-size cookies for school lunches.

Best of all, I like to have my routine back and time for myself. Most moms share this sentiment, although a handful of parents dread the end of summer because they miss their children. To them, I say, "SNAP OUT OF IT!"

Room Mother Winterizes Holiday Party

Ever since my kids started elementary school—almost a decade ago—I've done my part as a room mother. I take my volunteerism seriously. After an hour in a rowdy, germ-infested, overheated classroom, I automatically pop two aspirin and drench my extremities in hand sanitizer. One of my most challenging jobs as a room parent is to plan the school holiday celebrations throughout the year, including the fall (formerly Halloween) party, the winter (formerly Christmas) party, and the Valentine's (still politically correct even though named after a saint) party.

This time of year, most parents are usually sensitive about respecting different religious beliefs and understand the need to keep the festivities wintry as opposed to Christmasy. Still, every December, I encounter one or two moms who try to sneak a little controversy into the agenda.

For example, they want to know what's the harm in paper plates with snow-covered pine trees. Nothing, I tell them, as long as the spruce isn't decked out with colored bulbs and a five-pointed star atop. (The Christmas tree, by the way, is a religious symbol of eternal life.) Likewise, I'd rather pin the nose on Frosty than Rudolph, just to be safe. For some people, other potentially offensive decorations might include wreaths, poinsettias, stockings, picture frame ornaments, angels, reindeer, elves, jingle bells, and of course, jolly Saint Nick, who is being criticized these days for exclaiming "ho-ho-ho" in shopping malls. Candy canes, as long as they aren't tucked inside a felt elf's boot, are still considered okay. Gingerbread houses usually get the green light as well. The general rule of thumb, even for Jews, is that if it's edible it's kosher (not technically speaking, of course).

My goal, therefore, is to try to keep the winter party as neutral as possible. For example, I try to incorporate snow into everything. For a snack, powdered sugar donut snowballs. For a craft, paper snowflake cutouts. For the game, wrap the teacher in toilet paper so she looks like a snowman, I mean snowperson. For the goody bag, chocolate anything. Again, nobody cares as long as it's chocolate.

Finally, when the party is over, the excited students grab their coats, collect their candy, and shove their sticky art projects into their backpacks. Then the intercom buzzes and the principal announces, "Merry Christmas everyone! See you next year!" Yep, it's time to go home.

Valentine Parties Get To The Heart Of The Matter

Valentine's Day always makes me feel nostalgic. I can't help but harken back to my elementary school days, when I decorated a Stride Rite shoebox to collect my valentines. There were no holographic stickers, washable markers, and glittery gel pens in those days. To make my box pretty, I used red construction paper, pink hearts, and white paper doilies that I stole out of my mother's dining room hutch. I drew my name with a crayon, slit an opening in the cardboard lid, and, voila, created a work of art that cost my parents nothing more than a bit of aggravation over Elmer's glue on the kitchen table.

Back then, Valentine's Day school parties were a special treat. Everyone got a token of affection, even the misfits who got picked on at recess. In the public school districts, for the most part, nobody paid attention to any religious aspect of Saint Valentine's Day. Likewise, candy conversation hearts that read "Kiss Me!" and "Be Mine!" were never, ever, misconstrued as sexual harassment, not even by goofy pubescent fifth graders. In those days, candy was candy, you know what I mean? The worst that happened is we bit down on the hard-as-rock, pastel-colored confectionery and the sugary mess stuck in our molars for days.

Then again, our world was different then. We weren't living in a society with such fervent religious diversity, blatant sexuality, and political correctness. Over the last couple of years, depending on the decision of the individual principals, many of the rules have changed when it comes to school holiday celebrations, and Valentine's Day is no exception. At my daughter's school in Rockwood, for example, the theme of love and sweets has been replaced with friendship and cardiovascular awareness.

As a room mom, I should've seen this one coming. After all, our children are no longer allowed to dress like ghosts and clowns and parade in the hallways on Halloween. Instead, they celebrate the fall season with leaf-shaped sugar cookies and pumpkin bingo. Same with the winter parties—there's no discussion of Christmas, Hanukkah, or Kwanza. It's all about snowflakes and ice fishing.

And now Valentine's Day, which legend has it might have been named after an imprisoned man who fell in love with his jailer's daughter and sent her a love letter signed "Your Valentine" before he was put to death, is erased from the curriculum. Even Cupid, which comes from the Latin word for *cupido*, or "desire," is a mystery unless you study Roman mythology. Cupid and his buddy Eros, the Roman god of erotic love, mischievously wounds both gods and humans with arrows, causing them to fall in love.

So to play it smart and safe, many local public and private schools take advantage of the month of February to teach a lesson on health and community involvement. They promote activities like Jump Rope For Heart, which is a national educational fund-raising program sponsored by the American

Heart Association. While students engage in the physical benefits of jumping rope, they also collect money from family and friends to support lifesaving heart and stroke research. With more than nine million overweight children in the United States, the new emphasis on fitness makes sense, I guess.

Plus, Jewish schools are following the same trend at Valentine's Day, focusing on the heart of the matter. Then again, Jewish education has a culture all its own. Students don't exchange valentines or necessarily wear red clothing for Valentine's Day, but they don't ignore the holiday either.

For many of us, the best part about having Valentine's Day on the calendar is another excuse to eat chocolate and, of course, say, "I love you."

First Day of School Ritual

The older I get, the more I feel that life is on fast forward, and the pause button on the reality remote control doesn't work. For example, how can it be back to school time already when I barely have tan lines? Even though summer is not officially over, it sure feels like it when bags of Halloween candy crowd the store shelves that are still scattered with rejected spiral notebooks and two-pocket folders.

This school year is a particularly sentimental one. It's hard to believe that Jack is in ninth grade and starting his first year of high school. It seems like only yesterday when I slipped an orange Scooby Doo backpack over his shoulders and sent him off to preschool with a tear in my eye. And now he's enrolled in a drafting class with fellow classmates who have visible facial hair. It's scary.

In many ways, I'm a new high schooler all over again trying to find my own way. After the first parent orientation, I eagerly signed up for as many volunteer opportunities as possible, reminding myself of a classic episode of *The Brady Bunch* when the naïve, overly ambitious Marsha Brady joined every club on her first day at Westdale High. I want to be involved in my son's school and get to know his friends and the other moms. So far, this week alone I'm scheduled to sell sweatshirts in the school store, decorate the gym for the freshman dance, take pictures at the pep assembly for the yearbook committee, direct traffic in the parking lot, and scoop mashed potatoes in the cafeteria at lunchtime if the kitchen staff is short handed. And I will do all this and much more while I proudly wear my new wardrobe that has been gradually transformed into my son's school colors—black and gold.

I also encourage Jack to be active in school and meet new people. I expect him to pull straight A's while he participates in sports, the freshman advisory group, student council, ultimate frisbee club, Animal Welfare Alliance, Amnesty International, and marching band even though he doesn't know how to play an instrument.

Even my daughter Sari, now a fifth grader, embarks on a new journey as she enters her last year of elementary school. It hit me when I realized that colored markers were no longer on her school supply list. I bought a fresh pack of crayons anyway, in case she gets the urge to color at home. She is growing up so fast and is almost as tall as I am. What happened to my little girl? At recess she and her friends don't run around like they used to because they don't want to sweat before lunch.

Because time slips away so quickly and my children are transforming into young adults before my nearsighted eyes, I try to preserve every milestone in their lives. On the first day of school, for example, I always take their picture in front of the Chinese maple tree in the front yard. They don't argue with me anymore about it. They simply smile for the camera and click, it's done.

On the first day of school this year Sari wore her hair in a side ponytail and her outfit was color coordinated right down to the yellow tennis shoes. Jack's cargo shorts were oversized and wrinkly, as usual, and I didn't even notice that his blue t-shirt was inside out until he actually left for school. (I hope his reversible attire becomes a new style.)

Most families have a first day of school tradition. Every year I watch my neighbor chase the big yellow bus down the street with a video camera. Not only that—this mom follows the bus all the way to school and keeps the camera rolling as her children get off, walk into their classrooms, and wave goodbye on command. If I tried that with my own they'd never speak to me again.

So with the kids back in school, I settle into my routine. It feels good to have some time for myself. Then again, time slips away so quickly.

In front of the Chinese maple, Jack on first day of high school, 9th grade, August 2009.

Sari first day of middle school, 5th grade, August 2009.

Chapter 11
Teenagers. Need I Say More?

Teen Brain Baffles Parents

Being a teenager is tough, and so is parenting one, especially in today's fast-paced, high-tech world where, for the first time, kids are the ones teaching us about social media and how to navigate our way into the future. Honestly, without their help, I'd never figure out how to operate the remote or add new contacts into my cell phone. Teenagers consider themselves masters at multi-tasking. They do homework while they watch television, text their friends, play on the computer, and listen to music, all at the same time.

"It helps me relax and focus on my studies," said 15-year-old Jack, who used to collect baseball cards and now accumulates apps on his iPhone.

Whatever.

Let's face it. It's challenging enough for moms to endure premenopause without having to deal with the raging hormones and mood swings of their growing children. I feel sorry for husbands. I really do. I just hope mine doesn't add a mid-life crisis to the mix anytime soon. As long as we have enough Stridex and chocolate in our house to boost everyone's dopamine (the feel-good hormone) my family will get through this challenging stage called adolescence.

The transformation from child to adult is complicated, to say the least. To begin with, puberty starts younger than ever, between ages eight and 12 for girls and between nine and 14 for boys. I'm convinced the growing-up process lasts until they marry and reap the same grief from their own children. Some call it karma; the Rabbis call it *tzar gidul banim*, the Hebrew phrase for the inevitable pain of raising children. Seriously, if we as parents appreciated all the physical and neurological havoc that happens inside our children as they prepare for their *b'nei mitzvahs*, we would be in awe of them, really.

As neuroscientists discover that a crucial part of the brain undergoes extensive growth and change during puberty, adolescence can make the terrible twos seem like, well, child's play. For example, the same characteristics of a toddler—stubborn, impulsive, self-centered, emotional, rebellious—resurface in later years in teenagers. Only this time when a teenager throws a temper tantrum, a timeout is no longer a valid discipline.

Our babies are growing up. They no longer hang onto our legs like little monkeys; instead they hang out with their friends at the mall. They no longer run into our beds because they had a bad dream; instead they lock themselves in their own bedrooms and we can't tell if they're dead or alive.

They no longer read Eric Carle board books; instead they read trash on the Internet. They no longer call us on the phone;

instead they text us, if we're lucky. They no longer play Hi Ho! Cherry-O on family game night; instead they play video games with virtual strangers. They no longer socialize with their pals in the backyard; instead they socialize with their friends on Facebook. They no longer wake up at the crack of dawn; instead they want to sleep all day. They no longer give lots of kisses and hugs; instead the only one who gets their affection is the family dog.

For generations, adults have pondered the mystery of the American teenager. Hormones? Rap music? Boredom? Drugs? Violent video games? Overbearing Jewish mothers? Pictures of naked models on Abercrombie bags?

In order to better understand why teenagers act the way they do—and this includes the annoying habit of trying to match black shorts with a blue t-shirt—parents need to literally get inside their teenager's head. Good luck with that when their ear buds blast Lady Gaga and block any contact with the outside world.

With the aid of new technologies like MRIs, researchers are finding evidence that the brain is actually under construction for decades. The vast majority of brain development takes place in two basic stages. The first stage is called "blossoming," which occurs in utero and throughout the first several months of life. During this time, the human brain grows at a lightning-quick pace and produces millions of brain cells.

The second wave occurs roughly between the ages of 10 and 13 and is quickly followed by a "pruning" process in which the brain breaks down its weakest and least used connections. A favorite phrase of neuroscientists is "neurons that fire together wire together," explained David Walsh, Ph.D., a nationally renowned psychologist and author of the highly acclaimed parent survival guidebook, *Why Do They Act That Way?*

This is my favorite book when it comes to understanding teenagers, and I've highlighted every page in orange. It explains how if teens are involved in music or sports or academics, those are the cells and connections that will be hardwired. If all they do is lie on the couch and watch television or play video games, those are the cells and connections that will survive. The brain cells used most during puberty and adolescence are the ones that will become hardwired and most used in adulthood, so unless their future career is inventing the latest video game for Nintendo, they're wasting their time. This "use it or lose it" principle rationalizes why parents should introduce their children at an early age to the concept of helping others so that community service becomes a way life, which is the Jewish tradition of *tikkun olam*.

As adolescents physically grow into their adult bodies, their nervous systems are still very immature. So what exactly is going on inside a teen's *kepala*? To start with, fireworks explode in the prefrontal cortex (PFC), which is the part of the brain located just behind the forehead and is key to understanding adolescents. The PFC, by the way, is the last brain area to develop.

No wonder why smart kids do stupid things. Here's a perfect example: Last summer my son was staying at a hotel with his high school baseball team for an out-of-town tournament, which can get rowdy at times. A few guys decided to pull a seemingly harmless prank on the coaches. The 16-year-old ringleader (not my son) devoured a couple of fiber bars and then proceeded to poop in a paper bag. It gets worse. He microwaved his own excrement, broke into the coach's hotel room, and left behind the foul smelling evidence before he narrowly escaped down the hallway. Needless to say, the culprit was caught and suspended for the rest of the season. Apparently, this dude hasn't adjusted to his onslaught of new brain cells. Either that or he really is stupid.

Another area of the brain that experiences rapid change is the amygdala, which is associated with emotional and gut responses. New imaging studies suggest that teens interpret emotional information with this reactive part of the brain whereas adults rely more heavily on the more thinking regions in the frontal cortex. Scientists speculate that this may explain why teens have trouble modulating their emotional responses. In other words, when my daughter Sari, almost 12, has a hysterical fit because she can't find her Uggs and accuses everyone of hiding them, I blame it on her amygdala.

A new teenage chapter begins: Jack, 16, and Sari, 12, March 2011.

Still another puzzling piece of adolescent behavior—sleep— really hits a nerve for many parents. It turns out that their melatonin—the hormone that helps regulate sleep—is out of whack. My son, for instance, is a nocturnal hamster. He is wide awake at night and sound asleep on a pile of cedar chips all morning. The fact that many teens play on Facebook and video games in their rooms before bedtime doesn't help the situation.

So what does all this mean to parents? Most importantly, how can we motivate our teens to throw their wet towels in the laundry basket as effortlessly as they dunk a basketball into a hoop?

Thousands of years before the Positron Emission Tomography (PET) scans and other powerful machines were invented to study the brain, the wise Jewish scholars foresaw the best way to deal with teenagers. In the Talmud, for instance, the centuries-old advice on modern family dynamics is written, "Be it your way to thrust him off with the left hand and draw him to you with the right hand." In other words, practice tough love, baby.

Despite all the new scientific advances, researchers suggest that the most beneficial thing for teenagers is family support and a loving relationship with their parents. Even though our teens seem to push us away, they want us to be there for them. The developmental task of a teen is to begin to separate from their parents and connect with us in a more adult way. It's our job as parents to provide structure, guidance, and help keep them on the right track as their brain undergoes major construction.

Finally, I'll know my job is done when my teens grow up to become independent adults. Then again, I'll always be their mom.

The Cell Phone Wars

The other day I'm in the neighborhood bakery—just looking, of course—and I notice several leftover Valentine's Day cookies marked half price. The heart-shaped treats are decorated "Be Mine" and "Cutie" in pink and white icing, but one stands out from all the others. This cookie has red icing drizzled with the words "Text Me." Seems innocent enough, but I'm actually sad about this reflection on our society. Are today's teens falling apart just like the stale cookie crumbling next to the cherry stolen? Disheartened, I leave the pastry shop with a cup of coffee and a piece of glazed donut from the sample plate.

Cell phones (and donuts). We can't live with them; we can't live without them, and our tweens and teens are no exception. According to a national Harris Interactive study titled, "Teenagers: A Generation Unplugged," four out of five teens—that's 17 million—carry a wireless device, a 40 percent increase since 2004.

The problem is that every youngster nowadays, starting as early as elementary school, feels entitled to a cell phone. Raising kids is difficult enough without having to worry about the overuse and abuse of cell phones, not to mention the electromagnetic radiation they emit.

Granted, cell phones come in handy for safety reasons, such as when my daughter hangs out at the mall and needs to reach me. The question we need to ask ourselves is: Are they responsible and mature enough to use the device in a safe way? When Sari turned 12, all she wanted for her birthday was a cell phone.

Sari: "All my friends have a phone, so why can't I?"
Me: "If your friends jump off a cliff does that mean you'll jump too?"
Sari: "Huh?"

That argument seemed to work better when my own parents used it on me, then again so did "Eat everything on your plate. Children are starving in China."

So my husband Scott and I cave in and we make a deal with her. We compose a contract that spells out the rules and consequences for using a cell phone. If the written agreement is broken, she loses her cell phone for a certain amount of time. By the way, these types of contracts, which apply to driving a car as well, can be easily downloaded from the Internet, but that's our little secret. Tell your child you came up with the idea yourself.

Here's an example:

Cell Phone Agreement Between Parent and Tween

I know that having a cell phone is a privilege. I respect that my parents love me and want to keep me safe. My parents respect that I'm becoming a young adult and want the privilege of having a cell phone. With that in mind, we agree:

I won't go over the number of minutes, text messages, etc. (unless our plan is unlimited—woo hoo!) or consequently I'm grounded for a week and I have to wear whatever outfits to school my mom picks out.

I know that I'm required to contribute to the cost of my cell phone. My contribution is the amount of dollar bills that I negligently leave in my jean pockets and my mom finds later in the washing machine.

My cell phone must be turned off at bedtime or else I'll make everyone in the house really mad when they awake at 6 a.m. to the ringtone of Lady Gaga's "Poker Face."

I agree that if I'm unable to keep up with my responsibilities, such as feed the dog, empty waste baskets, and turn in my homework on time, the use of my cell phone can be taken away from me and I'll be forced to do laundry, make dinner, vacuum the steps, clean toilets, and run errands with my mom on weekends.

I won't use my cell phone to take pictures of nudity, violence, or other inappropriate activities that will wind up on Facebook and ruin my reputation and any chance I have of getting into the National Honor Society or a decent college.

I won't use my cell phone to call anyone for malicious purposes, such as bullying, pranking, or ordering Domino's pizza.

I won't use my cell phone while driving, especially when I don't have my driver's license yet.

I'll limit the amount of people who have my cell phone number to less than the quantity of my Facebook friends.

I'll limit the amount of time I'm on the phone to six hours a day, which means I need to talk and text fast. I won't use my phone while I'm sleeping and dreaming about phone accessories.

I'll turn off my phone during school hours or eat lunch in the principal's office for the rest of the school year.

I'll practice proper cell phone etiquette, such as turn the phone to vibrate during movies and High Holiday services. I will not bring my cell phone to the family dinner table and will not text my friends when they're sitting next to me on the couch.

I understand that I'm responsible for knowing where my phone is, unlike my mom who loses her phone and car keys at least three times a day.

Signed _____ (Tween)

Signed _____ (Parents)

Date _____

OMG! I'm RME @ TXT QSO

Kids seem to speak their own language. They always have; they always will. After all, young people sort of share the same tongue, and some of them pierce their tongues as well, but that's another fad.

Sari calls her girlfriends at school her "BFFs" (Best Friends

Forever), and Jack constantly tells me, "TMI" (Too Much Information), whenever I have to explain any kind of bodily function. Even the overused, full-of-attitude word, "Whatever," is shortened to just "WE."

The latest style of "QSO" (conversation) seems innocent enough, but these abbreviations are actually derived from an even more bizarre communication called text messaging. This text-based lingo twists the alphabet into secret codes that encourage "KPC" (Keeping Parents Clueless) and causes lots of "CSG" (Chuckle, Snicker, Grin) toward anyone who doesn't get it.

Meanwhile, I continue "RME" (Rolling My Eyes) because I can't keep up with all the changes in today's so-called social interaction. I guess I better "GAL" (Get A Life). Then again, I'm a "n00b" (Newbie) at text messaging.

Did you know that instead of "BYOB" (Bring Your Own Beverage) to a "PRT" (Party), it's more commonplace to say "BYOC" (Bring Your Own Computer) or "BYOP" (Bring Your Own Paint, as in paintball)? This is strange to me. Not only that, as soon as I catch on to the expression, "Been There, Done That," it shrinks to "BTDT."

Because of the popularity of cell phones and computers, young people have found a new way to converse that goes way beyond "ASAP," "TGIF," and "FYI." "AAMOF" (As A Matter Of Fact), it's amazing that anyone knows how to spell at all anymore.

Let's face it. Kids today are "AATK" (Always At The Keyboard), whether they like the immediacy and compactness of the new communication media for recreation or education. Plus, their modern dialect allows them to talk "A3" (Anytime, Anywhere, Anyplace) via instant messaging, e-mail, online chat rooms, discussion boards, and cell phone text messaging, even during *bar* and *bat mitzvah* parties.

Text messaging sounds so impersonal, but it doesn't have to be. To convey humor, users can choose from "OTFL" (On The Floor Laughing) or "LQTM" (Laughing Quietly To Myself) and "GOL" (Giggling Out Loud). The letter combinations go on and on. To apologize for something, users type in "IMS" (I Am Sorry) and to convey sadness, there's "555" (Sobbing, Crying) or "CLAB" (Crying Like A Baby).

For lack of nothing better to do, a "G/F" (Girlfriend) can send "143" (I Love You) and "H&K" (Hugs And Kisses) to her "B/F" (Boyfriend) because she is "BOOMS" (Bored Out Of My Skull) or "ZZZZ" (Sleeping or Bored) during math class. To save someone's life, good advice would be "ST&D" (Stop Texting And Drive). When tired of the whole thing, it's time for a "CB" (Chat Break).

Teens need their privacy, which is why parent alert codes are widely used, including "9" (Parent Is Watching),"AITR" (Adult In The Room), "MOS" (Mother Over Shoulder), "P911" (Parents Coming Into Room Alert), "PAW" (Parents Are Watching), and "PSOS" (Parent Standing Over Shoulder).

If text chat isn't weird enough, standard keyboard characters and punctuation also are used to express emotions, called emoticons. For example, to show a smiley face, a colon and a close bracket is used in the sequence that looks like the facial expression. The colon is the eyes and the bracket is a sideways smile. It looks like this :)

If you tilt your head to the left, you'll see what I mean. Still don't get it? Then a kid would assume "AYSOS" (Are You Stupid Or Something?).

Emoticons are important because the little symbols illustrate the sender's mood and intent. For example, "GAL" with a smiley face is meant as a joke and "GAL" (Get A Life) without one is supposed to be rude.

Typically though, most teens are all about manners and use "THNQ" (Thank You) and "YW" (You're Welcome) to show their appreciation. Likewise, they practice their social skills with "EMFBI" (Excuse Me For Butting In) or "PMFJI (Pardon Me For Jumping In) when they want to add ".02 MY" (My Two Cents) in a "P2P" (Peer To Peer) dialogue.

Of course, text messaging can be a legitimate communication tool for parents who want to ask their child "RUOK" (Are You Okay?) or if their youngster will "BHL8" (Be Home Late). Then again, in my day, I would simply pick up a phone and call my mom.

Bottom line, parents need to educate themselves about text chat lingo, such as "420" (Lets Get High, as in Marijuana) and the Internet world in general, including how to protect a child from online predators and cyber bullying on blogs, such as MySpace. Parental control software is another option for keeping track of what a teen is doing and with whom.

Chapter 12
Jews Don't Camp,
Except At The Hollywood Hyatt

Jewish Girls Don't Camp: Part 1

As if the Jews didn't suffer enough for the last several thousand years, I volunteered my family for our first real camping trip through my son's Boy Scout program at school. My intentions were, in part, a well-meaning attempt to dispel the old adage that Jewish girls don't camp.

Despite protests from my husband, who is more comfortable with a computer than a compass, and ridicule from my mother, who hassled me, "What are you, crazy?" I was determined to take advantage of this perfect opportunity to bond with my children in the great outdoors.

Since many aspects of Judaism stress the importance of being one with Mother Nature—*Tu Bishvat*, for example—I wanted to make this camping adventure a religious experience. So did Scott, who prayed everyday that I would change my mind.

I convinced myself that we could all benefit from a change of scenery and surely we could survive 24 hours in the woods. After all, we were surrounded by a pack of den leaders and every one of them knew how to utilize those mysterious gadgets hidden inside a pocketknife. As a devoted Scout mom, I figured the least I could do was sacrifice the comforts of home for one day so that my son could earn more arrow points.

Little did I know that our outdoor overnight would make Camp Sabra seem more like Club Med. To this day, I'm still afraid to zip myself into a sleeping bag. If only I had paid attention to the warning signs—and there were plenty of them—I would have saved my family from the humiliation of being the only campers to sneak out of our tent before the crack of dawn and watch the golden sunrise from our heated minivan.

The first hint of trouble began before we even pulled out of the driveway. That's when my kids panicked that the batteries in their Nintendos might die during the two-hour drive to the campground. I solved that problem when I borrowed a handful of double-As from inside a remote control car that no one seemed to use.

The kids organized their toys and batteries in their backpacks, while I loaded the van with enough food and supplies to last all summer. I piled in pillows, blankets, sleeping bags, grubby clothes, coolers, ponchos, old tennis shoes, towels, baseball gloves, toilet paper, bug spray, flashlights, a frying pan, and enough kosher hot dogs to gag a grizzly. I woke up my neighbors as I banged around the camping gear, including a lantern, family-size tent, plastic tarps, a stove with propane tanks, and two inflatable air mattresses that I borrowed from a friend and had no clue how to use. To make more room, I contemplated strapping the kids to the roof of the Dodge Caravan.

As the morning fog lifted, I tried to remain calm when my neighbor, an experienced outdoorsman, waved another red flag in my face and informed me that camping is "miserable fun."

At last, we were ready to hit the road when the phone rang. I assumed that it was my mom in a last ditch effort to bribe me with an offer to baby-sit the kids if we changed our minds and stayed home. Instead, it was our den leader Christine on the line, and her voice sounded weak. She told me how she was up all night with the stomach flu, but she assured me that she would be okay as long as she stayed off her feet and consumed nothing more than over-the-counter medication. I tried to sound sympathetic, but honestly I was more concerned about how Scott and I would pitch a tent and build a fire without her.

When we arrived at our destination, the beautiful Lost Valley Lake Resort in Owensville, Missouri, I jumped out of the van and stretched my arms up to the beautiful blue sky.

"Now *that's* fresh air!" I declared before I realized I had forgot the Claritin. I yanked the video games from my kids' paws and pointed them in the direction of the hundreds of acres of wooded wonderland.

"Go collect firewood, and try not to poke out anyone's eye with a stick," I yelled to the screaming Scouts as they scrambled into the tall timbers. "And watch out for poison ivy!"

None of the other moms seemed to pay any attention to where their kids disappeared into the forest, so I pretended not to worry either. Everybody had a job to do, and it had to get done before daylight was gone. Scott was in charge of the tent, which continually collapsed around him, and I had the daunting task to unload all the stuff that I struggled all morning to cram into the van.

After all our hard work, we were starved and couldn't wait to sink our teeth into thick, juicy steaks and sweet potatoes smothered in butter and cinnamon sugar that cooked over the fire.

Unfortunately, the frozen meat and giant potatoes took longer than our rumbling bellies could stand, so we curbed our appetite with weenies on a stick.

After dinner, the dads grabbed their flashlights and the kids for a nighttime hike. Meanwhile, Christine and I hurried to clean up the food and crumbs before the raccoons made themselves at home. Now I get why everyone tied their trash bags to the middle of tree trunks.

I tried to relax on a log, but I was told to gather my family's bedtime clothes and toothbrushes before the pitch-black sky blinded us. The lantern came in handy as I crawled around the cramped tent to find sweatshirts, socks, and, most importantly, my library book *Appalachian Trails*, which I planned to read by flashlight.

When Scott and the kids returned from their adventure, they fell into the tent and dressed in layers for the chilly night ahead. For a few minutes, I actually felt very calm and comfortable, like I floated on a cloud. Unfortunately, the peaceful moment didn't last long because the air mattress was slowly leaking. When Scott whispered something to me about a hissing sound, I noticed cold air escaping his mouth.

"What kind of hiss-hiss-hissing sound do you mean?" I stuttered. "If there's a rattlesnake in our tent, I'm-I'm-I'm gonna die."

I tried not to let the kids hear my teeth chatter when I continued, "I can hear my mom say, 'I told you so,' when we are rushed to the hos-hos-hospital with venom poisoning."

The four of us were scared and huddled together to stay warm. We laid still, either frozen in fear or from the falling temperature outside. I heard another noise, what sounded like a wild animal tearing into the bag of potato chips that I negligently left outside our tent.

Then, I heard silence, all except for a faint but steady "whoosh" sound that came from a tiny hole in the air mattress beneath me. As I gradually sank to the cold, hard, rocky ground next to my frostbitten daughter, I knew in my heart that I had experienced "miserable fun" for the last time. I tried to stop the leak with a bandage from my first aid kit, but it was useless.

Throughout the night, I felt daddy long legs crawling all over me and I heard the strangest chirps, squawks, howls, and crunching leaves from the footsteps of God-only-knows-who, maybe an escaped convict. Plus, in the tent next to us, my girlfriend's four-year-old daughter cried all night long because her daddy forgot her binkie.

If that wasn't bad enough, my husband snored so loudly that I had to wake him up, and he swore he never slept a wink. I was embarrassed that our friends would hear him or, worse, someone would think he was a bear and attack him in his sleep.

By the time I nodded off again, my daughter woke up because she had to pee-pee in the teepee. Thank God we brought a portable potty chair so that we wouldn't have to walk a mile to the nearest bathroom. In desperation, I never thought I would stoop so low, literally, but I was ready to burst myself.

Finally, I couldn't make my family suffer one minute longer. That's when Scott and I decided to break the rules and get out alive...

Me, Jack, and Scott pose innocently next to the infamous tent before the nightmare begins, April 2003.

Jewish Girls Don't Camp: Part 2

It was the longest night of our lives. Even my eyeballs were cold, if that's possible. We all were tired, dirty, grumpy, and miserable as we laid on top of the deflated air mattress that covered the rocky dirt like a cheap tablecloth. I guess it was about 5 a.m. because the birds started to chirp and the sun was still half-asleep when I realized that my family was not cut out for camping after all.

My realization was confirmed when Sari told me that she felt sick and started to cough. Instinctively, I grabbed the nearest plastic grocery bag and held it in front of her. Only then did I realize how many s'mores she had devoured the night before. Gross.

Sari's sickness was my breaking point. I sermonized to anyone who would listen that the Jews had suffered long enough in history and so had my family on this nightmare campout. No Boy Scout badge was worth this torture and I was determined to escape from our nylon jail as soon as possible.

We frantically unzipped our tent and raced to our parked van that awaited us at the top of the hill like a five-star hotel. The morning dew made the ground slippery and I tripped over a hard-as-a-rock potato that had refused to cook at last night's dinner. I watched the leftover potato roll away like a forgotten casualty in a war zone.

When we finally reached the parking lot, my kids lunged into the van and clung to their comfortable upholstered spots. Immediately, Scott cranked the heater full blast. I was embarrassed that someone would hear the motor run, but I didn't care.

I stretched my stocking feet on the dashboard and grabbed my journal. I wanted to document the details of our disastrous camping trip right away because I knew I had enough material to publish a story. I jotted notes about the gorgeous reddish-orange ball that I watched from the dirty windshield rise above the pine trees. I fantasized about the nearest Starbucks while Scott clenched his teeth and gripped the steering wheel. Sari sat frozen in the backseat and stared straight ahead. Jack found his Nintendo in the glove compartment and was in another world.

If Scott had his way, we would have hit the road by now. Somehow I convinced him to stick it out, at least until after the pancake and sausage breakfast. Our eyes were glued to the mounds of nylon cocoons scattered throughout the campground like a weird alien invasion. We waited for signs of life. Nothing. I was afraid that everyone was frozen dead.

Finally, a burly Eagle Scout with a serious five-o'clock shadow crawled out of his tent and stretched his arms into the overcast sky. We turned off the engine and scrunched in our seats as we watched the den leader rub his arms and try to shake off the cold.

I felt like a voyeur as we hid in our vehicle and observed in amazement how the brave man gathered logs and twigs to build a fire. He poked the wood around and somehow made smoke signals. We waited until the fire was nice and hot before we stepped out of the van with our heads hung low. I felt kind of guilty as we warmed our bodies around his roaring fire without having done any of the work ourselves. Then again, my pride was long gone since I had desperately borrowed Sari's portable potty in the middle of the night.

Another campfire began to crackle and someone brewed a bit of heaven in a blue-speckled coffeepot. I debated how morally permissible it was to hop from one campsite to the next.

Finally, the morning sun began to thaw our bones. We peeled off our hooded sweatshirts and relaxed a bit while the kids played hide-and-seek in the forest. I actually began to enjoy myself for the first time, but Scott couldn't wait to go home. He was the last parent to put up his tent and the first one to take it down.

I thought about what I learned from my first camping experience—besides never put aerosol cheese in a cooler. I guess if I learned one thing, it would be to never pass up an opportunity to bond with my family in the great outdoors, as long as I have a comfortable bed to come home to. Or a heated minivan.

Mishegas Meets Hollywood: Part 1

I was in full party planning mode for Jack's *bar mitzvah*. Nothing could distract me from my to-do list. Suddenly, without warning, my party planning came to a screeching halt. That's when I found out that I was going to Hollywood (yes, that Hollywood!) for the trip of a lifetime.

It all started on the Monday before Valentine's Day, which is the typical countdown to whether my husband will end up in the doghouse or not. That's when I learned that I had been selected as the grand prize winner in a writing contest for In *The Motherhood*, a groundbreaking online comedy series starring the gorgeous and talented actresses Leah Remini, Chelsea Handler, and Jenny McCarthy.

Seven days later, Scott and I were on a plane heading to Los Angeles to meet the stars and experience the behind-the-scenes making of the story that I wrote on my family camping disaster (see that doozy above!).

The unique concept behind In *The Motherhood*, which is the brainchild of MindShare Entertainment, is that real moms, like you and me, submit over the Internet a few simple paragraphs about mom-focused topics, such as toddler tantrums, sibling rivalry, and other embarrassing real-life moments. Then, online readers and an advisory committee vote on their favorite entries.

Next, professional screenwriters bring to life the best stories in a series of innovative, short, scripted comical webisodes. More than 20 million viewers tuned in to watch the hysterically funny *In The Motherhood.* Needless to say, my ordinary suburban life as a stay-at-home mom (who never stays home) has been changed forever, or at least was for a few days. Here's how it all started:

So, one evening I'm about to whip up something spectacular again for dinner—a recipe that involves Rice Krispies cereal, over-ripe bananas, and skinless chicken breast—when I decide to check my e-mail again, a compulsion of mine. As I routinely delete a bunch of junk messages, I stumble across an e-mail marked "Urgent!" I open it and quickly skim the letter that explains how I'm invited to Los Angeles next week to see the taping of a show that is based on a story that I submitted to the *In The Motherhood* writing contest last year. I have less than 24 hours to accept my grand prize, which is sponsored by Sprint and Suave, and I'm required to notarize an affidavit that proves my identity to the promotional company in New York.

What??!! I can't believe what I'm reading. Surely, there must be a mistake because I never win anything. I figure there's a catch; I either have to buy a case of Suave shampoo and conditioner every month for the rest of my life or at least upgrade my cell phone to a Sprint BlackBerry in order to be eligible. This incredible prize also includes a three night's stay at the Hyatt on Sunset Boulevard, a makeover at Lukaro Salon in Beverly Hills, a photo session with a celebrity photographer, limo service, and some other surprise perks.

I reread the e-mail again out loud about 10 times. Finally, when the news about an exciting free vacation and a possible big break in my writing career starts to sink in, I scream, "No way! No way! No way!"

I try to catch my breath as my kids read the e-mail over my shoulder, and then we all scream some more. "No way! No way! No way!" Sari scrambles to find the phone underneath a seat cushion. "I'm calling daddy and telling him that you won a trip!" she exclaims. I overhear their conversation while I read each word of the e-mail another time.

"Daddy, guess what? Mom won a writing contest...Her camping story is going to be a movie...She is going to California in a few days...I can't hear you daddy because mommy is still scream-ing...What?...No, she didn't make anything for dinner..."

I ditch the *bar mitzvah* plans like a bad blind date and make a new list of things to do to get ready for my spur-of-the-moment getaway and sudden taste of fame. As the sleet outside my win-dow freezes the mailbox shut, I can't wait to soak up the warm, California sunshine. I waste no time and drag a heavy suitcase from the basement. I start to throw in clothing when I realize that my wardrobe needs some spring cleaning.

I ask a flight attendant, who I meet on Wednesday at my daugh-ter's Valentine school party, what women in California are wear-ing these days. She tells me anything short and tight. Yeah, like that's going to happen. I settle on a few cute blouses, flared jeans, a hot pink swing jacket, hoop earrings, a black patent leather handbag, and high-heeled sandals that I can barely walk in.

All this time I think I'm traveling solo, so I don't worry about who's watching the kids while I'm gone. Scott plans to stay home and bond with Jack and Sari. Then on Thursday, four days before I'm supposed to leave for my whirlwind holiday to the land of the movie stars, I find out that I can bring a guest. I debate whether to bring my husband or a girlfriend, but Scott gives me no choice. He needs a vacation as much as I do.

I call Scott at work right away and announce, "Happy Valentine's Day, honey! You're going to California! Now it's your turn to shop for a few nice dress shirts to go with your stonewashed jeans. By the way, who's taking care of the kids?"

Fortunately, Grandma Vicki and Grandpa Norman come to the rescue and offer to stay with Jack and Sari and schlep them to school and all of their activities. Meanwhile, I hurriedly put everything in order to get ready for my Hollywood debut. Plus, to prepare the grandparents, I type a detailed itinerary of my children's upcoming schedule and a comprehensive list of names, phone numbers, and addresses of their pediatrician, dentist, orthodontist, orthopedic surgeon, dermatologist, otolaryngologist, school principal, neighbors, close friends, miscellaneous emergency hotlines, and, of course, the veterinarian.

I feel like I'm making progress and start to get excited about meeting the actresses, especially since I'm a huge fan. Leah Remini was the star of the sitcom *King of Queens*. Chelsea Handler is the outrageous comedian, best-selling author, and host of *The Chelsea Lately Show* on the E! network. And Jenny McCarthy is famous in her own right and for bringing much-needed awareness to autism.

Whoa—if I'm really going to meet these celebs then someone pinch me now because I must be dreaming. Then a nightmare happens. Jack wakes up Friday morning with a mysterious rash. He is itchy from head to toe with red bumps all over his body. I freak out that he might have chicken pox. I'm even more worried that Scott has to stay home and I'll have to find my own way around Los Angeles International Airport.

I call the doctor and she tells me to bring Jack into the office immediately for a cortisone shot because his symptoms sound like an allergic reaction to his acne medication. She asks me if his tongue is swollen or if he has trouble breathing. "No, he seems fine, but I'm ready to pass out," I say in a panic over the phone.

As I silently drive Jack to the doctor's, I rationalize in my head that my trip to Hollywood isn't meant to be. Maybe fate is interfering with my plans so that I don't board a hijacked airplane or something. Instead of feeling happy, I'm stressed out and exhausted.

When we get into the exam room, Jack hesitantly drops his drawers and the nurse pokes a stinging needle into his buns. "Don't worry," she reassures both of us. "The quick-acting medicine will give him immediately relief."

Afterward, I let Jack miss school and drag him to Macy's so that I can buy myself new makeup and underwear. My embarrassed son, then 13, wishes he was in school detention instead of with me in the lingerie department.

When we get home, I overdose Jack with Benadryl so that he finally conks out and stops complaining. Eventually, I get into bed after midnight and fall into a deep, comatose sleep when Jack wakes me in the middle of the night because he feels even more miserable. Before my very eyes, his hives manifest into red splotches all over his body, eyelids, hands, and scalp. I give him more antihistamine and the next morning we schlep back to the doctor's office for the second day in a row.

I'm in a fragile state of mind as I grip the steering wheel and stare through the dirty windshield. I begin to cry quietly to myself when Jack notices tears rolling down my face.

"Are you thinking about my *bar mitzvah* again, mom?" Jack asks me. "Because if you're crying already, then you'll be a basket case when I'm on the *bimah*."

I chuckle as I pull into the parking lot and head to the pediatrician's office. As we sit in the waiting room, I warn Jack not to breathe in too deeply or touch anything because of germs. After looking at Jack's rash, the doctor prescribes a quick round of prednisone and is confident that the boost of medicine will do the trick.

With that crisis resolved, I feel a little guilty about leaving the kids, so I call a family powwow in our bed on Sunday morning, the day before we leave for Los Angeles. The meeting comes to order:

Me: "I just want everyone to know that we're all winners of the *In The Motherhood* contest."
Jack: "What are you talking about?" he mumbles from underneath a pillow.
Me: "Well, without you guys we wouldn't have gone camping and there wouldn't be a story."
Sari: "But you get to go to California with daddy. No fair."
Me: "Daddy and I deserve a little time to ourselves. Besides, we'll take you on a cruise this summer."
Scott: "What?! We have a *bar mitzvah* to pay for!"

Mishegas Meets Hollywood: Part 2

Before Scott and I leave for the airport, I check my purse one last time: tickets, camera, extra batteries, lemon drops, business cards, lip gloss, hand sanitizer, cell phone, and a blank notebook for autographs. I'm good to go. The only items missing are baby wipes and juices boxes, which, on this trip, I won't need.

The older I get, the less I like to fly. So when we board the 747 and walk to our seats in the very last row of the economy section next to the lavatory, I start to feel a little uneasy. Sure I have a window seat, but a gigantic wing completely obstructs my view. For the next several hours, I cover my head with a winter coat because the vibrating high-pitch roar of the airplane engine causes me to almost hyperventilate. Not even ginger ale calms my nerves. Still, Scott and I are looking forward to this trip of a lifetime, even if the flight attendant forgets to offer us peanuts.

When we finally arrive in Los Angeles, a chauffeur named Reynaldo waits for us at the baggage claim and escorts us to a luxury BMW right outside the door. After I settle into the plush leather seats, I roll down the window and take in the warm breeze and tropical palm trees. Like every tourist, I search for the famous Hollywood sign in the foggy distance. We weave through traffic and eventually arrive at our hotel on Sunset Boulevard in West Hollywood, where someone rushes to open the car door for me. I can get used to this.

Before I have a chance to unpack my toiletries, I'm sipping a tangy mojito and tipping a guitarist who serenades Scott and me with a soulful rendition of Stevie Nick's *Landslide*. Like Dorothy in the *Wizard of Oz*, I whisper to Scott, "We're not in Kansas anymore."

The next morning, a talkative driver named Steve, who claims that his regular clients include Mel Gibson, Drew Barrymore, and Leonardo DiCaprio's agent, whisks us to our destination. We are on our way to meet the cast and crew of *In The Motherhood* on location, which is at a fitness center in Burbank, California. When we pull into the parking lot, Steve opens the door for me and the driver and I exchange business cards (hey, I might be back!). I ask Scott to take a quick picture of the chauffeur and me together next to the black Lincoln Town Car.

On the set, I notice all the trucks, trailers, cameras, equipment, tangled electrical cords, and lots of busy people scurrying around with jobs to do. We meet our contact person, Marisa, from Mind-Share Entertainment in New York, which produces the show. She greets us enthusiastically and introduces us to her colleagues, including Greg, the executive producer, and David, the president of the worldwide media company and creator of the successful *In The Motherhood* campaign.

We take our seats in director's chairs, plug in our headphones, and listen and watch the famous actresses on the other side of the window say their lines and crack jokes between takes. I'm in awe of how Hollywood filmmaking works, especially when I'm so lucky to be a part of it on this day. We are told to whisper while the cameras are rolling, so I try not to laugh out loud.

Marisa asks if we're thirsty or hungry and offers us cake. People eat cake in Hollywood? I thought everyone's dieting all the time. Before we break for lunch, we actually get to meet the three stars of the show: Leah Remini, Chelsea Handler, and Jenny McCarthy, who are gorgeous, down-to-earth, and hysterically funny. I tell the talented trio that I'm a huge fan, and they probably think to themselves, "Stop kissing up to us. You already won the contest," but it's the honest truth.

We put our arms around each other and take a couple of pictures together. While the actresses retreat to their fancy RVs, Scott and I hang out with the fun gang from MindShare Entertainment and other friendly folks who work for Sprint and Suave, the sponsors of the series. By coincidence, I meet a dark-haired, blue-eyed girl named Jeanne, who is from St. Louis and went to my high school.

After we exchange, "No ways!" Jeanne gives us the scoop on lunch, which in the biz is called "craft services." We enjoy a delicious all-you-can-eat buffet of grilled fish, barbecued chicken, corn on the cob, salads, and cheesecakes. By the way, snacks are also provided all day long and include everything from fruit and candy to sodas and aspirin. We all sit together and eat at picnic tables under tents.

Everyone is casual and friendly and I don't even bother reapplying my lipstick when a cameraman from the television show *Access Hollywood* and a reporter from *In Touch Weekly* magazine stop me in the parking lot and ask me for an interview about winning the contest.

"Me? Are you kidding? You want to talk to me?" I nervously ask them as I turn around and look for the person I assume they are after. "What am I supposed to say? Do I have time to put on lip gloss?"

"Just be yourself," advises the guy with the microphone. Sure, like that's going to put me at ease.

After a few more hours of taping the first film, the crew packs up all the equipment and we share rides to another location miles away to shoot my camping webisode. This time we set up shop at the scenic Griffith Park in Los Angeles. The production company continues to ask me questions on camera and documents my step-by-step experience as the first mom invited to the set of *In The Motherhood*.

As evening approaches, the air turns chilly. I notice that the wooded acres are so fragrant with pine needles that I swear someone is spraying scented air freshener to get the actors in the mood. For most of the time, we sit in a comfortably heated tent and sip espresso while we watch on monitors how the adorable lead actress Remini delivers one sarcastic line after another, right on cue.

To get closer to the action, I sneak up a hill with my digital camera and watch how the director patiently sets up each scene. The sleeping bags, flattened tent, lantern, and the sound of crunchy leaves bring back memories of when my family barely survived our first overnight camping trip several years ago. In the familiar sketches when Remini and her daughter go wee wee in the woods, I feel honored to play a role in this comedy.

As if a full day of Hollywood filmmaking isn't enough excitement, the next morning Scott and I are treated to a makeover at the exclusive Lukaro Salon in Beverly Hills. A Suave representative named Sara escorts us to the Mediterranean-style building with the famous 90210 zip code.

Lukaro is the same salon that Brooke Shields, Luci Liu, and other movie stars trust for their locks, so we're in good hands. First, the manicurist paints my nails with the most fashionable Hollywood color, black-brown. Then, the makeup artist shapes my eyebrows perfectly and brushes blush on my cheeks. The next thing I know a celebrity photographer named Chris snaps my picture again and again and makes me feel like a celebrity. With every click of the camera, he tells me, "Life is good!"

Luke, the owner of the salon, trims my hair and blows it dry for a straight and slightly feathery style. My hair will never look this good again. Luke is magical with scissors and comb and his outgoing personality and charisma is as unique as his white splotch of hair that reminds me of a tamed Sweeney Todd wig. Luke works wonders on Scott, too, and gives my husband a handsome new cut and touch of color. Scott and I are all smiles as we pose for the zoom lens all over again.

We end up staying an extra day in California because our flight is cancelled due to an ice storm in St. Louis. We pack in another day of sightseeing, including visits to the Kodak Theatre, the Hollywood Walk of Fame, and we even squeeze in souvenir shopping at The Grove at Farmers Market.

Eventually, we say goodbye to Hollywood, at least for now, and are anxious to return home and see Jack and Sari again. It doesn't take long for me to get back into my routine of washing jeans with pens in the pockets, making creamed cheese and jelly sandwiches for school lunches, and opening my own car door. Even though my life is changed in some ways, it's still the same. One thing is different—the *Vanity Fair* Hollywood issue replaces *Real Simple* magazine on my coffee table.

Leah Remini, Scott, Me, Jenny McCarthy, and Chelsea Handler in Hollywood, February 2008.

Me getting pampered in Lukaro Salon in Beverly Hills, February 2008.

Me after my Hollywood makeover, February 2008.

Epilogue

I've been doing a lot of contemplating lately. In particular, I'm thinking about how much I'll miss the *mishegas* when Jack and Sari grow up and move out of the house. I'm also racking my brain to figure out where I put my cell phone—again. I've searched everywhere: my purse, my coat pockets, the front seat of the car, the garbage can, and even in the freezer under the cheese pizza. Seriously, I've found car keys in there before.

Anyway, when I gave birth to *Mishegas of Motherhood*, my biggest concerns were getting my children to make their beds, do a *mitzvah*, balance schoolwork and sports, appreciate their Jewish values, honor their mother and father, and chew with their mouths closed.

Now I'm entering an entirely new chapter in parenting—raising teenagers. And I thought planning a *bar* and *bat mitzvah* was challenging!

I've already started on Volume Two of *Mishegas of Motherhood*. It'll cover the high school and college years.

God help me.

The centuries-old wisdom of the sages got me through the early years of child rearing. I know that this same, sane advice will come in handy as I face a world of driving, dating, and who knows what else, because quicker than I can spin a dreidel, I'll join the lonely ranks of empty nesters. Don't even get me started.

Let's face it. We all want our children to grow up to become independent, loving, self-confident, ambitious adults who use their unique gifts to help make this world a better place, right? Of course, as long as they call their mother every night before they go to sleep in their college dorm and let me do their laundry when they come home to visit.

Remember, when it comes to parenting, keep the faith. After all, it takes a village—I mean a *kibbutz*—to raise a child. So let's kibbitz again soon.

Gotta go! I think I found my phone. The wastebasket is ringing.

Ellie S. Grossman
September 2011

ABOUT THE AUTHOR
Ellie S. Grossman

If stretch marks and caffeine addiction aren't sufficient enough qualifications to write a parenting humor column, Ellie S. Grossman actually graduated in 1986 from the University of

Missouri School of Journalism where she learned how to squeeze who-what-where-when-why-how into one lead sentence. Known by her readers as the "Jewish Erma Bombeck," Ellie is a freelance writer and stay-at-home mom who never stays home. Her stories have appeared in newspapers, magazines, and blogs across the country.

Photo by Lisa Mandel

This book is a collection of her most popular *Mishegas* of *Motherhood* columns, which offer an interesting combination of wit and wisdom when it comes to modern issues facing today's families. Her musings are inspired by her family, including her husband, Scott; her children, Jack and Sari; and her beloved apricot toy poodle, Luci, but not necessarily in that order. Ellie and her family live in St. Louis, MO.

Visit her at home, her homepage that is:
www.mishegasofmotherhood.com

CPSIA information can be obtained at www.ICGtesting.com
Printed in the USA
LVOW010150081011

249522LV00001B/4/P